I LIKE MYSELF

I Like Myself

Fostering Positive Racial Identity in Young Black Children

Toni Sturdivant, PhD

Published by Redleaf Press
10 Yorkton Court
St. Paul, MN 55117
www.redleafpress.org

First edition 2023
Cover design by Jesse Hughes
Cover photographs by adobe.stock.com
Typeset in Freight and Nunito Sans
Printed in the United States of America

30 29 28 27 26 25 24 23   1 2 3 4 5 6 7 8

Library of Congress Cataloging-in-Publication Data
Names: Sturdivant, Toni, author.
Title: I like myself : fostering positive racial identity in young Black children / by Toni Sturdivant, PhD.
Description: First edition. | St. Paul, MN : Redleaf Press, 2023. | Includes bibliographical references and index. | Summary: "This book provides lesson planning insights and academic activities that are designed to facilitate positive racial identity in Black children. Supplementing and complementing any curriculum, this critical resource provides information across social-emotional, academic, and fine arts domains that stay faithful to curricular goals while specifically targeting the racial identity needs of Black preschoolers"— Provided by publisher.
Identifiers: LCCN 2022049443 (print) | LCCN 2022049444 (ebook) | ISBN 9781605547893 (paperback) | ISBN 9781605547909 (ebook)
Subjects: LCSH: African American children—Education (Preschool) | African Americans—Race identity. | African American children—Social conditions. | Race awareness in children—United States. | Education, Preschool—Curricula—United States. | Affective education—United States.
Classification: LCC LB1140.3 S78 2023 (print) | LCC LB1140.3 (ebook) | DDC 371.829/96073—dc23/eng/20221019
LC record available at https://lccn.loc.gov/2022049443
LC ebook record available at https://lccn.loc.gov/2022049444

Printed on acid-free paper

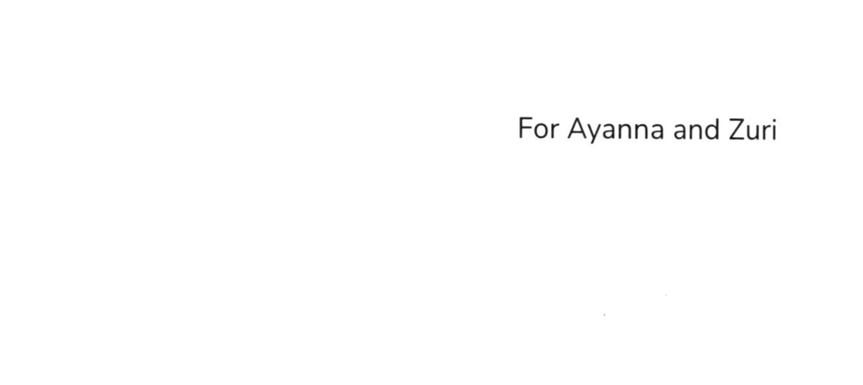

For Ayanna and Zuri

CONTENTS

ACKNOWLEDGMENTS

I would like to acknowledge Mamie Clark, whose vision and work set the foundation for my own. Additionally, I would like to acknowledge all of the faculty members who assisted me on my journey, especially Dr. Iliana Alanis. Finally, I would like to acknowledge Dr. Aisha White, Dr. Shannon Wanless, and the whole team at the P.R.I.D.E program at the University of Pittsburgh for assisting me in my research.

The Need for This Work

Teachers consider an incredible number of factors to plan just-right lessons for the children in their classrooms. Being an exceptional teacher means that we ensure student learning in many ways, responding to a variety of learning styles, abilities, and dispositions. Not only do educators have to teach standards, but we often create learning experiences that pull from the wealth of knowledge that our students, even the youngest learners, bring from home. Excellent early childhood educators plan their days based on student interests and include exciting, hands-on, joyful learning experiences with frequency. Being an impactful early childhood educator is a tough job, but it is incredibly rewarding.

We get to see children's faces light up with pride when they have finally learned a new skill. We celebrate when they make the connection between something they explored last week and a new experience this week. Children build a considerable amount of knowledge and skills during their early years, especially when we have taken the time to carefully plan for each of the children in our care.

I have seen this all firsthand, having spent my entire professional career in early childhood. I worked as a toddler teacher at a preschool during my undergraduate studies. While I was pursuing my master's degree, I was an instructional assistant at a school district–run Head Start center. Upon graduating and becoming a certified teacher, I served as a teacher of record at the same school, teaching three- and four-year-olds. From there, I became a master teacher for the city of San Antonio, working as a PreK–4 teacher in a model classroom with visitors from all over the United States stopping by our observation windows to see high-quality learning in action. The next part of my career took me away from the classroom full time. I became a professional learning specialist and coach, creating and facilitating trainings for early childhood educators working in school districts and early learning centers. I thoroughly enjoyed working with teachers and helping them become more effective in their practices.

Along with planning for standards, interests, and engagement, the most effective early childhood educators I've worked with also plan for the lived experiences of children and their cultural backgrounds, which include race and ethnicity. All people, including young children, bring their cultural ways of knowing and being with them. Exceptional early childhood educators see individual culture as an asset and an important source of information from which to build their teaching. Intentionally celebrating differences and using the cultures of students as a bridge to the social, physical, artistic, and academic skills we set out to teach each year is essential. But this is not enough.

Celebrating diversity teaches children that what is special to them and their family and community is also important enough to include in the classroom. However, messages about diversity are not always positive, especially for Black, Indigenous, and other People of Color (BI&POC). Messages of anti-Blackness can teach children with at least one Black biological parent (henceforth referred to as Black children) that the essence of who they are is a problem. Additionally, children who are not Black are also privy to these messages of anti-Blackness, which can lead them to believe all sorts of misinformation about Black people and Blackness as well as to believe their racial/ethnic group is superior. This can have devastating consequences.

Effective early childhood educators know that creating a warm environment that fosters a positive sense of self for everyone in the learning community is essential for supporting healthy development and ensuring learning success. Therefore, when we draw our attention to the Black children in our care, as we should for all of our children, we must celebrate aspects of Blackness and counter the messages of anti-Blackness that children inevitably receive that can harm their developing racial identities.

Typically, when educators and researchers discuss child development, the focus is on physical, cognitive, language, or social development. We hear far less about racial identity development. Even though it is left out of many conversations, racial identity development is profoundly important for Black children. Research shows that Black children who have positive racial identities, that is, children who see their inclusion in a particular racial group in a positive light, do better in school (Zirkel and Johnson 2016) and have better overall psychological well-being (Brittain et al. 2013). This is big! Put in another way, Black children who are confident in being Black tend to do better than their peers who do not feel the same way. This means that educators who care about the lives of children must also consider and plan for racial identity development, just as they do for other aspects of development.

The Advancing Equity in Early Childhood Education Position Statement by the National Association for the Education of Young Children (NAEYC) lists recommendations related to equity and diversity for many groups of stakeholders (Alanís, Iruka, and Friedman 2021). For early childhood educators, there are several recommendations, but there are two in particular that strongly align with fostering positive racial identity: creating a caring community of learners and countering common stereotypes and misinformation. As the authors explain,

> Create a Caring, Equitable Community of Engaged Learners. Uphold the unique value and dignity of each child and family. Ensure that all children see themselves and their daily experiences, as well as the daily lives of others within and beyond their community, positively reflected in the design and implementation of pedagogy, curriculum, learning environment, interactions, and materials. Celebrate diversity by acknowledging similarities and differences and provide perspectives that recognize beauty and value across differences. (xi)

In creating a caring community, educators work to make sure that all children feel they are supposed to be in the space. The children know that they can be their full selves and that they are not only accepted but celebrated for who they are. Fostering this feeling for all children is the ultimate goal of creating a learning community. However, for children from certain groups, their social identities, such as race or ethnicity, may make them not want to bring their full selves into the classroom. Some children might hesitate to celebrate aspects of themselves because the greater society outside of the classroom has influenced the way they feel about them. For this reason, simply celebrating diversity is not enough, and educators need to go a bit further. Iliana Alanís, Iheoma Iruka, and Susan Friedman (2021, xii) state that early childhood educators should also "counter common stereotypes and misinformation. Remember that the learning environment and its materials reflect what you do and do not value by what is present and what is omitted." Though it may not seem that young children are internalizing ideas about racial stereotypes and misinformation, research tells us that children pick up on racial information quite early. The next section explains further.

Racial Identity Development and Early Childhood

Not only is racial identity development important over a life span, but forming a positive racial identity is uniquely paramount in the early years due to how quickly children develop their sense of self. According to Christy Byrd (2012), racial identity includes:

- racial awareness
- racial identification
- racial attitudes

Therefore, to create a timeline of the development of racial identity, we should examine at which age each aspect generally begins.

Racial awareness is simply being able to notice differences in the ways people look when those differences would lead to being assigned to different racial categories (skin color, hair texture, and so on). Racial awareness is the first part of racial identity that develops, starting in infancy and getting more sophisticated over time. According to Paul Quinn and colleagues (2016), infants have racial awareness at three months of age. These researchers found that White and Black three-month-olds prefer to look at pictures of faces that match their own racial identity over others. For such a preference to exist, infants must be able to attend to racial differences. According to Erin Winkler (2009), six-month-olds can classify others based on race and gender, and toddlers are already using race as a way to make sense of the behaviors of others—for example, a toddler might believe that someone did something because they were Black.

Racial identification is being able to correctly name the race of oneself and others. Racial identification involves not only having racial awareness but also knowing the vocabulary used by the greater society to label different groups. Research dating back to the 1940s that has been consistently replicated shows that children as young as three are able to correctly identify their race (Clark and Clark 1947). Deborah Van Ausdale and Joe Feagin (2001, 48) observed four-year-old children referring to themselves and others as a "White person" and a "Black person." Additionally, they observed a White three-year-old who could not only identify the race of a Black classmate but also showed developing racial attitudes, or at least an awareness of racial attitudes around him, as he called her an n-word. Many studies have revealed the developing racial attitudes of young children and show that many had already internalized anti-Black beliefs about who is good, attractive, and desirable (Sturdivant 2021a and 2021b). These internalized notions of anti-Blackness, or negative racial attitudes, are common but also troubling because, according to Anna Hindley and Julie Olsen Edwards (2017), racial attitudes do not change much after age eight without a major intervention.

With my understanding of developing racial identity and young children, I was concerned because I knew from my experiences in classrooms that talking about race and ethnic differences in a real and meaningful way was not a common early childhood practice. I was curious to see if I would also observe children behaving in similar ways at a high-quality early learning center. My curiosity led to me designing a study in a preschool classroom.

My Research

To gain more information on the developing racial identity of young children, I conducted an observational exploration of racial identity development in Black preschool girls. For the study, I placed four dolls—two Black dolls (one with lighter skin than the other), a White doll, and a Latina doll—into the dramatic play center in a preschool classroom. For a semester, I observed the girls and their peers as they played with the dolls, and I discovered quite a bit about the racial learning of the students in the classroom.

The findings of the study revealed some key information about the developing identities of Black preschoolers. They showed a strong preference for light skin and for straight and long hair. The focus girls of the study not only wanted to play with the White and Latina dolls over the Black ones, but they also mistreated the Black dolls. Additionally, they pretended to beautify themselves by pretending to lighten their own skin and pretending to have long straight hair. These findings mean that these Black children preferred features unlike their own. They were learning to reject parts of their own identity in favor of the dominant group. This is a problem. The good news is that there was room for improvement in the ways the teachers handled race in their classroom. Unfortunately, their curriculum, which provided lots of hands-on materials for concrete academic learning, included books with only White or animal protagonists. While the teachers did not have the power to change the curriculum, they did get to engage in lesson planning. For this reason, I felt that a book that guided early childhood educators through this planning process would be a useful asset.

The Role of Educators

I Like Myself provides lesson planning insights and academic activities designed to encourage positive racial identity in Black children. Although this book provides information across the span of social-emotional, academic, and fine arts considerations for the early childhood years, it is not meant to replace current curriculums. I am aware that centers, schools, and districts spend a great deal of money on curricula materials. I am also aware that it is stressful for teachers to learn new curricula. For this reason, I have designed *I Like Myself* to complement any high-quality curriculum. This coupling allows teachers to stay faithful to their curricular goals while planning lessons that specifically target the racial identity needs of the Black and biracial children in their care.

Early childhood educators do not need to have a certain number of Black or biracial children to make the lessons necessary. This book is useful whether there is one Black student enrolled or Black children make up the majority of the students in the classroom. The approaches to lesson planning are aimed at providing engaging, meaningful, and effective lessons for all students while targeting Black identity specifically. If teachers incorporate similar activities targeting all of their students' identities, each child will walk away feeling valued and accepted while also gaining the knowledge and skills they need to be successful. This is the goal of quality early childhood experiences.

Educators have a powerful opportunity because research shows that the school context and the actions of teachers play a role in the development of racial identity (Escayg et al. 2017). As educators you already have an adopted curriculum and a set of standards or skills that you must teach. Instead of challenging you to do all of the things you are already doing and then adding another list of things on top of that, I would like to do two things. One is to offer you a few examples of hands-on and engaging activities for all of your students that can contribute to fostering positive identities in your Black and biracial students. The second, and arguably the most important, is to show you how to plan your own lessons that do the same.

Discussion Questions

1. What racial groups are visible within your current curriculum? Which cultural groups are visible in illustrations and visuals? In learning materials?
2. Whose perspectives and cultural norms are dominant in your current curricular practices? From what racial and cultural backgrounds are the authors of books included in your curriculum? Of the curriculum itself? Are children expected to behave in ways that closely align with White middle-class norms? (For example, requiring one speaker at a time instead of dynamic conversations or asking everyone to display calm demeanors instead of being animated during highly emotional times.)
3. How do your current curricula materials handle topics of diversity? Are diverse groups represented in authentic, humanizing ways or reduced to stereotypes? Are People of Color represented as important contributors to our society or as side stories? Are they mentioned at all? Does your curriculum teach children about resisting stereotypes? Handling racial microaggressions? Being confident in their racial characteristics?
4. When did you first encounter the term *racial identity development*? Why do you think racial identity development might be left out of child development courses? What steps can you take to make the development of racial identity a more widely known concept within early childhood?
5. With racial awareness beginning at three months and racial views nearly solidified by age eight, early childhood educators are uniquely positioned to change the trajectory of racial understanding in our society. What steps can you take to harness this power? Within a single classroom? Within a center? Within the broader community?
6. How do the children in your care currently play with diverse toys?
7. How do you feel about spending moments where Blackness is the focus? Why?

All about Afro Hair

CELEBRATING TIGHTLY TEXTURED HAIR

Within Eurocentric beauty standards, long, straight, flowing hair is perceived as desirable. Whether it is the main feature of a character in a major children's movie, the focus of a shampoo commercial, or the only representation of beauty found in the aisles of the grocery store, stereotypical European hair texture is widely celebrated. This glorification can be detrimental to Black children, as their hair is often nothing like the images that bombard us. In my own study, I found that the preschoolers, both Black and non-Black, were very much resistant to the dolls with the Afro-textured hair, some even explicitly saying that they did not want to play with the dolls with big or curly hair (Sturdivant and Alanís 2021; Sturdivant 2021b).

The children in the classroom made their negative feelings toward Afro hair known in ways other than rejecting the dolls. One student also asked me to change my hair, while another student said her Black classmate's hair was crazy. A separate child who was wearing her hair in braids said that she would have to take her braids down soon or else her mom said her hair would get too curly, and another saw a picture of an Afro and said she wanted her doll to have beautiful hair, as opposed to what she saw in the picture. The children also spoke of media images that celebrated Eurocentric beauty standards, from television shows to movies, and mentioned costumes based on these characters. It was clear that the children in the classroom had internalized messaging from a variety of sources that Afro hair was unpleasant.

Fortunately, many children's books celebrate Afro-textured hair. Just as the students had accepted the negative messages, with consistent and meaningful counter messages, the children could learn to see the beauty in other hair textures.

Supporting Research

Because it can be difficult to receive permission to do research with young children, especially about race, there are few research-based examples of children grappling with the topic. However, one way researchers can still gain some understanding of what is happening is to ask parents. In interviews of parents of young children, researchers Idara Essien and J. Luke Wood (2021) uncovered some disturbing information. Parents said that both their young children's peers and their teachers made negative remarks about their children's hair. They found that when Black children with kinky hair wore their hair naturally, families were met with criticism and pressure from teachers to straighten their child's hair. Parents reported that other young children teased their children for their hair. An example follows:

> My daughter came home and said that a little White boy had teased her about her hair. She had her hair in braids with a bun and had just put some fresh oil on them. He said to her, "Why is your hair so dirty?" It hurt her feelings. She said, "My hair isn't dirty" and he said, "Yes, it is, I wouldn't say it if it wasn't true." She says that he is ALWAYS mean to her. (8)

In addition, parents of children with one non-Black parent reported being praised by teachers for their child's "good" hair. This praise, though well-meaning, cannot be a compliment since it comes from the same Eurocentric standards of beauty that critique the more tightly coiled hair of one parent as well as the other Black children in the classroom.

Researchers Afiya M. Mbilishaka and Danielle Apugo (2020) interviewed Black women about the role of hair in their schooling experiences and found that these women reported experiencing shaming based on hair texture and length from peers and teasing from teachers, similar to the findings of Essien and Wood (2021). Though my study took place in a different setting and involved different children, I likewise witnessed children saying harmful things about Afro hair texture and length. Therefore, although the findings are disturbing, they are not shocking.

We want all children to go to school and be confident in themselves so they can grow, develop, and learn. Being teased and shamed impedes these crucial activities in early childhood. Fortunately, early childhood educators can take steps to help prevent Black children from having these sorts of experiences. The next section highlights some activities and practices used by early childhood educators that specifically target feelings about Afro-textured hair.

Real Examples of Good Practice

Hearing about research findings that demonstrate the struggles of Black children in schooling can be disheartening. Thankfully, there are educators doing the work to help ensure these sorts of experiences will one day be a thing of the past. Each of us can improve our practice by learning from the work of others. This section focuses on some promising actions educators have taken to foster positive feelings about Afro-textured hair.

Kristen Kemple, Il Rang Lee, and Michelle Harris (2016) acknowledge that young children see physical differences that get sorted into racial categories (hair, skin, and so on) and at times they are vocal about these differences, but they contend that teachers can be proactive in leading positive discussions about differences to mitigate harm. They argue for including read alouds on topics such as hair and for early childhood educators to engage in discussions about the books in their classrooms. The researchers suggest that educators foster conversation through acknowledging children's responses and correcting any misinformation, repeating what a child has said, and then extending their language and asking children to use the new words introduced in the extension.

As early childhood educators, we can take care to select books that showcase the beauty of kinky, coily, and curly hair as well as the diversity of hair in general. After the reading, we can then engage in conversations following the previously detailed approach to acknowledge children's natural curiosity about difference, foster positive racial identity in Black children, and help teach all children how to talk about differences without inflicting harm on others.

Shannon B. Wanless and Patricia A. Crawford (2016) detail a scene in which an early childhood teacher was playing with children in the dramatic play area, pretending to style the hair of the classroom baby dolls. She followed up on this play experience by reading *I Love My Hair!* by Natasha Tarpley, illustrated by E. B. Lewis, and ended with a discussion of what caregivers do to take care of the many types of hair people can have. Similar to what Kemple, Lee, and Harris (2016) presented, using books as a springboard to have conversations about hair texture, length, and care made what could have been a difficult conversation to facilitate more natural for the educator.

Along with reading books, Aisha White and Wanless (2019) offer other promising practices: having conversations, creating a positive physical environment, and allowing children to talk about their own experiences. Effective early childhood educators already engage in two-way authentic conversations with their children. We can add healthy conversations about hair to our repertoire of topics. The physical environment sets the stage for future learning, as educators pay attention to the representation of hair lengths, colors, and textures in the toys, displays, books, and other materials in the classroom. Finally, teachers can be proactive in helping children develop the skills to stand up for themselves in the face of shame or taunting from peers.

It is common to walk children through using their words or using big voices for conflict situations, such as taking turns, sharing, or maintaining personal space. There is no reason why early childhood educators cannot also teach children how to use their words or big voices to assert that their hair is perfect just the way it is. We must address these common sorts of conflicts so that Black children are not victimized without being taught what they can do to defend themselves.

Practical Solutions to Celebrate Afro Hair

To help to foster positive racial identity development, we must regularly integrate topics that feed into racial identity into the early childhood classroom. It is not enough to do one read aloud followed by a conversation, set up the physical environment, and engage in a large-group activity that teaches students to stand up for themselves. While all of the ideas from the field could easily be implemented in a variety of learning settings, to be fully committed to fostering positive racial identity, each educator must continuously plan related experiences. First I will take you through some steps to help you plan your own lessons that tackle negative views of Afro-textured hair, and then I will leave you with some specific activities that you can customize for your classroom today.

Countering negative messaging with activities is a two-step process. The first step is to think about the content of the negative messaging surrounding Black people's hair. Looking over the research and from lived experience, I can say that key areas are **hair length**, **hair texture**, **hair styling**, and **hair care**.

After identifying the specific messages to counter, the second step is planning ways to address the harmful messages through teaching and activities. I recommend two basic approaches to combining academics and messages about racial identity; first, identify curricular areas that naturally lend themselves to this topic, and second, use a book as a springboard. The message is more likely to be received when educators address these ideas while also targeting academic standards so that facilitating positive identity does not become separate from everyday teaching.

The idea that good and healthy hair is long, especially for girls and women, is problematic for two reasons: (1) many Black people's hair does not grow long when compared to other racial groups, and (2) it can be almost impossible to examine the true length of natural Black hair as it greatly shrinks when it has not been treated by heat. Therefore, to address potentially harmful ideas surrounding hair length, teachers can plan how to talk about varying lengths of hair as valid and beautiful. Questions of length pair readily with activities about measurement. While planning an activity where children measure each other's hair would technically combine the two topics, it does not actually counter the anti-Black messages around hair length. Because long hair is already more widely praised, simply measuring hair would mean that some children would leave feeling bad about themselves. Instead, the goal is to counter this idea. This is a fundamental difference between simply celebrating diversity (hair length) and planning targeted experiences to counter negative societal messages. Therefore, instead of measuring hair, students could measure other things to demonstrate that length is not that big of a deal. Keeping this in mind, educators can offer everyday items that vary in size but still serve the same function, such as shoestrings, children's books, blocks, and other toys. Depending on the age of the students, the class can work together, or children can work individually to measure objects and then report how long they were (ten paper clips long, four sheets of paper long, and so on). Follow up this math experience with a discussion about how the various lengths do not make a difference in functionality or style but it is just a difference, just like our hair. This sort of activity can be repeated with different objects on different days to ensure the message has gotten across.

The second part of the hair length problem is that Afro hair shrinks up when it gets wet, so unless the hair was blow-dried after being washed, the visible length is a shrunken version of the hair. This change in hair length due to water and heat lends itself to a scientific exploration of the properties of matter. Just like with length, instead of planning an activity based specifically on hair shrinkage, educators can use other materials and then relate the experience back to hair. Wool that has not been chemically treated also shrinks when it is wet. A science exploration at the sand and water table with wool socks from a secondhand shop would be a perfect example of this phenomenon.

Hair texture is also a common issue, with hair that is most unlike the straight ideal preferred the least. For this topic, a book is a useful springboard because the concept of texture is so specific to hair, and it is difficult to plan activities to show how the type and size of coils and curls should not matter without actually using hair. Because the book itself is focusing on hair, the activity accompanying the reading does not necessarily have to do so.

For example, *I Love My Hair!* features a character who discusses getting her hair styled with beads. Beads are a staple in most early childhood classrooms. Educators can read the book and then engage children in a bead-related activity, reminding them of the beads that were put into the little girl's Afro hair in the book. This same book also touches on the other negative messages related to Afro hair: hairstyles and hair care. Teachers can point out the many different hairstyles that Keyana wears in the book and how her favorite style, the Afro, also happens to be the hairstyle that children and teachers alike have been shown to have the hardest time accepting. Early childhood educators can share this hairstyle preference research with children in the form of a story or through a puppet show that makes the words from the adult article you read come to life in a way emergent readers can experience and understand. Remember the child mentioned previously who told the Black girl her hair was dirty because it was oily? This book addresses that piece of misinformation as the mother adds oil to her daughter's hair to style it. Coconut oil changes states depending on temperature. Try a science exploration with coconut oil sealed in a bag: it starts off as a solid, melts as children handle the bag, and then becomes a solid again when the bag is placed in a bowl of ice. While this experiment is engaging for a variety of early childhood age groups, it can also help non-Black children understand why their peers' hair may appear greasy.

Looking beyond *I Love My Hair!*, educators can select a variety of books that authentically celebrate Black hair and then use the books' events and themes to plan follow-up activities that target the general goals and standards of the classroom.

To recap, to uplift Afro hair, educators should counter four areas from which misinformation arise: **hair length**, **hair texture**, **hair styling**, and **hair care**. Each of the four ideas can be approached in two ways: (1) planning an activity that is not about hair specifically but can relate back to an idea about hair, and (2) reading a book out loud that authentically and positively discusses Afro hair, then designing a lesson, not necessarily about hair, based on the content of the book.

Using these two approaches, educators can plan engaging experiences with books and materials they already have available at their site. For educators looking for more examples, the following section includes ready-to-implement lessons and experiences that follow the outlined steps. Each activity is separated by age group, but keep in mind that there is a great overlap in what can be done in each stage of the early childhood classroom and that activities presented in the infant section can also be adapted for a toddler or preschool classroom.

Celebrating Hair with Infants

Learning in an infant classroom includes lots of singing and short read alouds, along with mirror play. Each of these learning scenarios can send positive messages about hair diversity and celebrate tightly textured hair or Afro hair. Here are a few practical ideas that you could implement in your infant classroom tomorrow.

Songs

"I Love My Hair" (sung to the tune of "Twinkle, Twinkle Little Star")
I love my hair; yes, I do.
I love my hair; so should you.

Curls and coils, kinks and 'fros,
In a puff or with some bows.
I love my hair; yes, I do.
We love our hair; so should you.

"Hair Like a Cloud" (sung to the tune of "Mary Had a Little Lamb")
Hair that looks just like a cloud, like a cloud, like a cloud
Hair that looks just like a cloud is just the hair for me.

Hair that spirals like a shell, like a shell, like a shell
Hair that spirals like a shell is just the hair for me.

Hair that looks just like a wave, like a wave, like a wave
Hair that looks just like a wave is just the hair for me.

Hair that looks just like long grass, like long grass, like long grass
Hair that looks just like long grass is just the hair for me.

"All Hair Is Great" (sung to the tune of "The Itsy Bitsy Spider")
There are all kinds of hair that can grow out from a head.
Some hair is black or brown, some is blonde or red.
Some hair is kinky, curly, waved, or straight.
No matter what hair you have, all hair is great.

Read Alouds

Short board books make for great read alouds in an infant classroom. Regardless of the book, educators must use their voices and mannerisms to engage babies and keep their attention. A board book that specifically celebrates Afro hair is *Cool Cuts* by Mechal Renee Roe, which focuses specifically on hairstyles traditionally seen on Black boys. The same author has a companion board book entitled *Happy Hair* that features Black girls.

Mirror Play

It's a common practice to include infant-height safety mirrors in our youngest classrooms. Infant teachers can use the moments when infants are enjoying their reflections to talk about hair texture and color in a positive way. We often point out other things, like the colors of their onesies or the smiles on their faces. We can use this same approach to say uplifting words about the many textures of hair found in the room.

Hair Play with Toddlers

When someone walks into a toddler classroom, they will hear songs, hear read alouds, and see children in mirrors, so all of the information from the infant section still applies. To those experiences we add sensory play, dramatic and pretend play, and lots of counting, so the ready-to-implement ideas for toddlers focus on these areas.

Sensory Play

Educators can allow toddlers to experience different textures by filling empty tissue boxes with interesting items to feel. To relate this activity to hair texture, select items related to different hair textures, such as cotton for Afro hair; braided or twisted yarn for braids, twists, or even locs; curled ribbon for curly hair; and strips of paper for straight hair. This sensory experience could also be turned into a matching game: toddlers are given pictures of Afro, braided, curly, and straight hair and encouraged to match the pictures to the box with items that feel similar to each hair type.

Black Identity-Centric Salon Play Props

In addition to the play props typically included in salon play (mirrors, hair bows, combs, brushes, and so on), including items that are widely used by Black-identifying families will enable Black children to role-play the types of styling situations that they observe and experience in their homes and communities and also let non-Black children learn about their peers.

- Afro picks
- wave brushes
- rat tail combs
- edge brushes
- boar bristle brushes
- Black hair magazines
- empty hair oil bottles
- empty hair gel jars
- empty leave-in conditioner jars
- wooden beads (large)
- nonworking hair dryers with comb/brush attachments
- pretend makeup that includes dark brown foundation colors

Some Supporting Books

Happy to Be Nappy by bell hooks, illustrated by Chris Raschka
Don't Touch My Hair! by Sharee Miller
Princess Hair by Sharee Miller; *Happy Hair* by Mechal Renee Roe

---

Dramatic Play

Encourage hair-related dramatic play by providing props to play hair salon with dolls. Educators can structure the experience in a way that does not allow children to refuse or mistreat the Black dolls, for example announcing each "customer" and allowing the toddlers to choose between two hairstyles for that doll. The children can then attempt to style the doll's hair into the style. Books are a great source for hairstyles.

Some Supporting Books

Happy Hair and *Cool Cuts* by Mechal Renee Roe

Early Math: Counting

Black hairstyles use many hair accessories: beads, bows, ribbons, barrettes, small hair ties, clips, beaded ponytail holders, headbands, and more. Any of these items can be counted, sorted by color, lined up by size, and so on. Choose items that are large enough to not be a choking hazard for toddlers.

Some Supporting Books

I Love My Hair! by Natasha Tarpley, illustrated by E. B. Lewis
Happy Hair by Mechal Renee Roe

Addressing Standards through Hair in Preschool

Preschool should be a fun and playful time filled with singing, sensory play, read alouds, dramatic play, and counting games, so the lessons from the previous sections still apply. In the midst of the play and exploration in preschool and prekindergarten classrooms, there are more teacher-directed experiences. For this reason, the preschool ready-to-implement ideas focus on two learning domains: math and science.

Math

Classification and patterning: Bead patterns. Children can work on patterning skills by threading hair beads on string or yarn to create a patterned design similar to what we see on braided hair. Use the skill level of each child in creating patterns to decide how many colors of beads to give them, with more advanced students given more colors. Children with an oral fixation can be given large beads to prevent a potential choking incident. Providing beads of different shapes and sizes allows children to make patterns by shape and size too.

> **Some Supporting Books**
>
> *I Love My Hair!* by Natasha Tarpley, illustrated by E. B. Lewis
> *Happy Hair* by Mechal Renee Roe

Counting: Matching numerals to puffs. Educators begin by writing the numerals 0–9 on index cards, making several sets so each child in a small group gets their own. Students also need pictures of children wearing their hair in different numbers of Afro puffs. For example, a picture of a child wearing her hair in a single Afro puff would match with the numeral 1, a picture showing a child wearing her hair in three puffs would match with the numeral 3, and so on. This activity becomes even more meaningful if educators can include pictures of their actual students, but this is not necessary. This activity allows children to associate quantities with numerals. Children could also match numerals to the number of rows in cornrows, plaits in plaited hair, or twists in a twist hairstyle, to use a variety of common Black hairstyles to teach quantity.

Some Supporting Books

Hair Love by Matthew Cherry, illustrated by Vashti Harrison
Happy Hair by Mechal Renee Roe; *Princess Hair* by Sharee Miller

Geometry: Shaving cream shapes. Barbershops and shaving cream go hand and hand. Use cans of shaving cream to cover the tables and invite children to use their fingers to create shapes. This common multisensory activity is a lot of fun, and when paired with a read aloud about Black hair and the barbershop, it becomes even more meaningful. Using shaving cream for sensitive skin will help avoid irritating children's hands.

Some Supporting Books

Crown: An Ode to the Fresh Cut by Derrick Barnes, illustrated by Gordon C. James
Cool Cuts by Mechal Renee Roe

Science

Life science: Classifying hair texture. In this science exploration, teachers take pictures of the back of each child's hair. The students then use their eyes or even a hand lens to observe the differences in hair textures. After observation, the students work together to group the various hair textures into categories. This science activity can be linked with a graphing math activity. First, the children could group the hair by texture, and then they could graph it as a separate activity. However, this classification activity can be completed as a stand-alone activity as well.

Some Supporting Books

Princess Hair by Sharee Miller; *Happy Hair* by Mechal Renee Roe

Physical science: Water beads. In *Hair Love* by Matthew A. Cherry, illustrated by Vashti Harrison, Zuri mentions how water causes her hair to change. Educators can remind their students of this as they introduce this water beads exploration. Water beads grow once they have been submerged in water. Give each child a small cup of water beads and a small cup of water. When everyone is ready, direct the children to put their water beads in the cup of water. Allow the children to draw and "write" their observations. After some time has passed, have the children check in on their water beads. What has changed? Let them document the changes and discuss them.

Physical science: Texture scavenger hunt. Educators prepare for this activity by creating a scavenger hunt sheet that includes words and pictures of different textures children will look for. Some possibilities for textures include *smooth*, *rough*, *bumpy*, *soft*, and *hard*. Each child needs a scavenger hunt sheet and a writing utensil to mark off the textures they find. Then children use their sense of touch to search for the textures in the classroom, throughout the school, or outside. They can report their findings to the group or a peer once the hunt has ended. Tip: Laminate the scavenger hunt sheets and give children washable markers so the activity can be used over and over again.

Some Supporting Books

Happy to Be Nappy by bell hooks, illustrated by Chris Raschka
Princess Hair by Sharee Miller

Discussion Questions

1. What kind of experiences, positive or negative, do you think the Black children in your care are having regarding their hair? Why?
2. What are your feelings about naturally kinky hair? How might this affect the Black students in your care?
3. What are your feelings about loosely curled hair on Black children? How might this affect the Black students in your care?
4. What sorts of lessons or activities could you plan that relate to hair length? Hair texture? Hair care? Hairstyles?
5. What are some titles of books that celebrate Afro hair that you own already? What are some you could check out of the library or purchase?
6. Looking at the curriculum, learning guidelines, or standards for the children in your care, which topics or skills could pair well with a book or discussion about hair diversity surrounding hair length, hair texture, hair styling, or hair care?
7. How can your coworkers, colleagues, or administrators support you in your quest to counter negative messages about Afro hair?

Comfortable in My Skin

SHOWCASING THE BEAUTY OF DARK SKIN

Like hair texture, skin color has long been a way to rationalize how we treat people or assign worth. Of course, this should not be the case, but it is the reality of our society. Unfortunately, children are quite apt at picking up on societal messaging, and, as such, show racial bias in their play. Children in preschool have been shown to mistreat peers based on skin color, treat toys differently based on their coloring, and say mean things about someone's race or ethnicity. This hard-to-swallow reality can be detrimental for Black children, as they have the physical characteristics that are being rejected and are often the victims of mistreatment.

In my study, I saw children use play makeup to pretend to lighten the skin of Black dolls as well as their own. Instead of being silent about differences, adults who care about how children with darker-hued skin see themselves and people like them must take action and consciously celebrate dark skin. We must acknowledge the messages that are getting through to young children and then make sure we are doing our part to counter harmful or negative sentiments about certain groups of people.

Supporting Research

According to research conducted by Danielle R. Perszyk, Ryan F. Lei, Galen V. Bodenhausen, Jennifer A. Richeson, and Sandra R. Waxman (2019), preschoolers had both an implicit (internal, unspoken) and an explicit (verbalized) pro-White bias. Black boys were seen in a more negative light than Black girls, but all Black children were perceived more negatively than both White boys and girls. Sixty-three percent of the children in the study were White, while the non-White children (Black, Asian, Latino, and multiracial) accounted for 37 percent of the participants. Viewing Black children in a more negative light both implicitly and explicitly likely means that these children have displayed behaviors that show off their beliefs. As young children base their racial categories mostly on the color of one's skin, rather than other physical features (Dunham et al. 2015), this pro-White bias can manifest as bias against darker skin tones. The work of Caryn Park (2011, 402) shows us that young children are very much aware of differences in skin color and categories, as she describes children sorting through flesh-toned coloring utensils to find the exact right shade. A White child explained that a shade was too "blackish" to match his own, and other children freely spoke of their skin tones, hair colors, race, and ethnicity when asked by a puppet. Unfortunately, there was also evidence of race-based social exclusions, as White students rejected or refused to play with various children of color. According to Park, the physical environment of the preschool classroom was quite diverse, but there was adult silence about racial differences, despite the children spending time talking about skin color among each other and with the researcher. Other educators have taken steps to try to mediate anti-Black beliefs about dark skin tones; the following section shares a few of those practices.

Real Examples of Good Practice

Preschool teachers often use paint mixing as an entry point to talk about skin color and race. After students mix paint to make their skin tone and name their color, teachers and students can have conversations about how colored racial terms (Black, White) describe people with a range of skin colors. The teachers in a 2016 study (Kuh et al.) took this experience a step further and invited families to come into the classroom to mix their own colors and discuss race. In Patricia Sullivan's research (2020), a preschool teacher at a nature school explained how she felt taken aback when a Samoan student said a crow was bad because it was black. After a series of art activities aimed at investigating the children's views of Blackness, which were overwhelmingly negative, the teachers created a unit to learn about crows and celebrate the color black. Shannon B. Wanless and Patricia Crawford (2016) described a classroom activity that began with a child talking about a new baby sibling. The early childhood teacher followed up by reading a book celebrating diverse skin tones, which led to a discussion of what babies look like.

Early childhood educators use art, children's books, and nature as springboards for countering negative beliefs about dark skin tones. These examples from the field are a start to openly having discussions about race; however, to foster positive racial identity, these sorts of activities should be common in early childhood classrooms. For this reason, I have provided more resources in the sections that follow.

Practical Solutions for Celebrating Skin Tone

Due to notions of colorism—the idea that lighter skin tones are superior or preferable to darker skin tones—addressing skin color bias means understanding how our society has a skin color hierarchy. Understanding this helps to guide where the primary focus of activities should be. The correct mix of celebrating all human colors generally and celebrating specific hues of skin entails critically thinking about which messages need to be heard the most—or to put it another way, determining which messages are currently heard the least. Early childhood educators can help balance society's messages by focusing on what is so often neglected. Practical solutions to this problem must include an awareness of the anti-Black skin color hierarchy that we have been exposed to and a desire to eradicate it.

If whiteness is currently at the top of our society's color hierarchy, then we need to pay close attention to ensuring that (1) dark skin tones are celebrated and (2) dark colors, in general, are seen as valuable. As we noticed in the crow conversation, prevailing messages about the negativity of darkness in general intersect with our ideas about skin color. Early childhood educators can address both issues to help ensure positive racial identities for their students.

Educators can celebrate dark skin tones in various ways, by (1) celebrating all skin tones, (2) focusing on darker hues specifically, (3) discussing why we have differences in skin tones, and (4) celebrating people with dark skin tones. Each of these four concepts is critical in fostering acceptance for dark skin tones, and all must be balanced to ensure that the focus is not too heavy on one area and not another. Children's books remain an important and easy-to-implement means to ensure that all four components are covered. Luckily, there are published children's books focusing on all of the components.

Many books celebrate the beauty of different hues of skin: *All the Colors of the Earth* by Sheila Hamanaka or *The Colors of Us* by Karen Katz are two. Early childhood educators can read these or similar books and engage in conversations about differences. Additionally, paint mixing activities celebrate all skin hues.

When it's time to focus specifically on darker skin tones—since they are perceived to be at the low end of the hierarchy and thus need dedicated attention—other children's books can spur classroom discussions. Some include *Lullaby (for a Black Mother)* by Langton Hughes, illustrated by Sean Qualls; *I'm a Pretty Little Black Girl!* by Betty K. Bynum, illustrated by Claire Armstrong Parod; and *Sulwe* by Lupita Nyong'o, illustrated by Vashti Harrison.

Discussing the reasons why we have different skin colors in the first place also helps combat anti-Black messaging regarding skin color. *All the*

Colors We Are: The Story of How We Get Our Skin Color by Katie Kissinger discusses the science behind skin color diversity and how families, geography, and melanin play a role in our skin colors. The book easily links to topics beyond skin color, such as different kinds of families, places where people live, and life science. Integrating racial content into "academic" areas shows how important the topics are as well as how they relate to the greater world outside of the classroom.

The Little Leaders series make the accomplishments of Black people, women, and other People of Color accessible to young children. From author and illustrator Vashti Harrison come the hardcover books *Little Leaders: Bold Women in Black History*, *Little Dreamers: Visionary Women around the World*, and *Little Legends: Exceptional Men in Black History*, as well as three board books for young children: *Dream Big, Little One*; *Think Big, Little One*; and *Follow Your Dreams, Little One*. Each of these texts, along with many other biographies written specifically for young children, foster positive feelings about Blackness through a celebration of Black people. Find more detail about the importance of celebrating Black people and characters in chapter 6, which focuses specifically on representation.

The other side of planning to celebrate dark skin colors is fostering positive feelings about dark colors in general. Art activities in which only dark colors are available, such as painting with black and brown paint, as well as children's books aimed to celebrate the color black, such as *Black Is a Rainbow Color* by Angela Joy or *Black Bird Yellow Sun* by Steve Light, or color songs like the ones provided in the infant section next are all ways to do so.

Tuning into Skin in Infant Classrooms

Because we know that infants attend to racial differences, we must start sending our youngest learners positive messages about human diversity and messages designed to counter anti-Blackness. In an infant classroom, we have the power to spread positivity perhaps before negative messaging has become internalized. What an honor! Sticking to mirror play, songs, and read alouds using board books, as in chapter 2, the following sections detail some suggestions for addressing skin color with infants.

Mirror Play

As with hair texture, infant teachers can positively highlight skin color differences during mirror play and exploration. Affixing color swatches that closely resemble human skin colors to mirrors can encourage children to explore color diversity as they are looking at themselves. Affirm skin tones through mirror play by taping butcher paper to parts of the mirrors and giving the babies edible natural paint so that they can explore with nature colors while also looking at themselves in the mirror.

Songs

"Here's My Skin" (To the tune of "This Old Man")
Here's my skin.
It covers me.
I have skin from my face to my knee.
We all have skin; it doesn't look the same.
Dark skin, light skin, there's no shame.

"Lots of Pretty Colors" (To the tune of "She'll be Coming 'Round the Mountain")
People come in lots and lots of pretty colors.
People come in lots and lots of pretty colors.
Some have dark skin; some have light skin.
Some have brown skin; some have beige skin.
People come in lots and lots of pretty colors.

"Dark Skin" (To the tune of "I'm a Little Teapot")
Dark skin is great skin; yes, it is.
Dark skin is great skin; yes, it is.
People who have dark skin are great people too.
Many have dark skin; how about you?

Brown skin is great skin; yes, it is.
Brown skin is great skin; yes, it is.
People who have brown skin are great people too.
Many have brown skin; how about you?

Light skin is great skin; yes, it is.
Light skin is great skin; yes, it is.
People who have light skin are great people too.
Many have light skin; how about you?

Read Alouds

A few board books that focus on skin color are *The Skin You Live In* by Michael Tyler, *I Am Mixed* by Garcelle Beauvais and Sebastian A. Jones, and *Shades of Black: A Celebration of Our Children* by Sandra L. Pinkney. When selecting books for read alouds, educators can focus on any of the important messages related to skin color: celebrating all colors, focusing on dark skin, showing how we get our skin colors, or celebrating people with dark skin as well as celebrating dark colors in general.

Additionally, assess the books in your classroom that teach about colors to ensure that the dark colors are not being associated with negative items, as this reinforces anti-Blackness rather than countering it.

Color Study with Toddlers

In addition to the activities, books, and songs mentioned in the infant section, toddlers can also enjoy skin color–based sensory play, matching activities, and group art activities.

Sensory-Based Play

Toddler teachers can put a sensory spin on the skin tone paint mixing activities. Let toddlers choose the human skin tone paints that they want to put into a sealable plastic bag. Then portion the paint into the bags, seal them up, and allow children to squeeze and mix the paint inside of the bags. Children can use their new paint colors for painting human cutouts that are then displayed in the room to represent the diversity of skin tones. Teachers can paint human cutouts as well to help ensure that darker skin tones are represented in the display.

Some Supporting Books

The Skin You Live In, by Michael Tyler, illustrated by David Lee Csicsko
I Am Mixed by Garcelle Beauvais and Sebastian A. Jones, illustrated by James C. Webster
Shades of Black: A Celebration of Our Children by Sandra L. Pinkney

---

Matching Activities

Target fine-motor skills and boost an appreciation for different shades of brown by using paper paint sample cards (such as from a paint or hardware store) to make a clothespin matching activity. Take two copies of the same paint sample card that displays multiple shades of brown. Cut one card into four and affix each individual shade to its own clothespin. Then place the clothespins and the intact paint sample card together in a bag or basket.

Toddlers can match the shades of brown on the clothespins to the whole paint sample card. While toddlers are completing the activity, teachers can comment on the characteristics of each shade of brown.

Some Supporting Books

The Skin You Live In, by Michael Tyler, illustrated by David Lee Csicsko
I Am Mixed by Garcelle Beauvais and Sebastian A. Jones, illustrated by James C. Webster
Shades of Black: A Celebration of Our Children by Sandra L. Pinkney

Group Art

I always enjoyed making class murals with my students. I would roll out a piece of butcher paper and place it on the carpet. Each child had their own space to work, and at the end of the lesson, we would have a large piece of collaborative art to display in the hall or somewhere in the classroom. This experience can be related to skin tone as well. Provide each toddler with a large nontoxic glue stick and give them shades of brown and black paper, magazine clippings showing various skin tones, and any other art materials you see fit. At the end of the experience, teachers can display the artwork that celebrates dark colors and diverse skin tones. Any book about skin color or color books that positively portray dark colors can support this activity.

Some Supporting Books

The Skin You Live In, by Michael Tyler, illustrated by David Lee Csicsko
I Am Mixed by Garcelle Beauvais and Sebastian A. Jones, illustrated by James C. Webster
Shades of Black: A Celebration of Our Children by Sandra L. Pinkney

Centering Skin in Lessons with Preschoolers

Preschoolers will enjoy and benefit from the songs, read alouds, art, fine-motor, and mirror play activities mentioned for younger children. Preschoolers, though, can typically go even further in exploring color.

Science

Life science: Nature walk. Many books about human skin color differences describe shades of brown with beautiful descriptive language. A read aloud about the shades of human skin could be extended to include celebrating brown in other parts of nature. Preschool teachers can take their class on a nature walk to look for different shades of brown. Students can write down their observations and share them with the class, a small group, or a partner.

Some Supporting Books

The Colors of Us by Karen Katz
All the Colors of the Earth by Sheila Hamanaka

Physical science: Shadow puppets. Children can explore light and darkness through shadow puppets. Teachers start by shining light on a blank wall and demonstrating how to create a couple types of shadow puppets. Then they let children explore by creating and naming their own shadow puppets. Connect the concept of shadow puppets to the theme of this chapter by emphasizing how the shadows exist because of both light and darkness working together.

Some Supporting Books

Sulwe by Lupita Nyong'o, illustrated by Vashti Harrison
Lullaby (for a Black Mother) by Langston Hughes, illustrated by Sean Qualls

Life science: Be melanin. For this whole-body movement activity, preschool teachers need cards with different skin colors on them and a music playlist with songs of various tempos. In the book *All the Colors We Are: The Story of How We Get Our Skin Color,* author Katie Kissinger explains variations in skin hues by how active someone's melanin is. Start by reminding children of this fact and tell them that they will move their bodies more quickly for colors that have more active melanin and more slowly for colors that have less active melanin. Hold up a color with more active melanin and play an up-tempo song that allows the children to move quickly. Then hold up a skin color with less active melanin, and play a slow song so children move slowly. Play songs that are neither fast nor slow for mid skin tones.

Another Supporting Book

M is for Melanin: A Celebration of the Black Child by Tiffany Rose

---

Math

Counting: Spot the number. Continuing to honor the importance of both light and darkness, teachers can use glow-in-the-dark wall and ceiling decals to engage in a fun counting activity. Write numerals on glow-in-the-dark stars and then affix them to the ceiling. Then, turn off the lights, invite children to lay on their backs, and call out numbers for them to seek on the ceiling. If putting the stars on the ceiling proves to be too difficult, affix them under tables. Just make sure the stars have adequate time to absorb light so that they will glow once the lights are turned off.

Some Supporting Books

Sulwe by Lupita Nyong'o, illustrated by Vashti Harrison

Lullaby (for a Black Mother) by Langston Hughes, illustrated by Sean Qualls

Counting: Counting bodies. As students are engaging in conversations about skin color, body parts inevitably come up. We know our skin through our body parts. Young children can practice counting objects by counting the number of parts of their bodies. Educators can direct children to count how many legs they have, fingers, noses, feet, necks, and so on. Additionally, students can count how many of some parts they have altogether in their classrooms, keeping in mind the class's ability to count. For example, counting the total number of fingers in the classroom could be too much depending on the group, but you could count the number of heads in the room or maybe even arms.

Some Supporting Books

The Colors of Us by Karen Katz
All the Colors of the Earth by Sheila Hamanaka
Sulwe by Lupita Nyong'o, illustrated by Vashti Harrison

Measurement: Measuring height. Many children's books that discuss human diversity in skin tones also mention other ways we differ from each other, such as shape and size. The children in any classroom are also different shapes and sizes—this is what makes measuring height so fun! To do this activity, educators need yarn and scissors. Have each child (in a small group) stand up and cut a piece of yarn that is the same height as they are. Then tape each piece in one part of the room, labeled with each child's name. The children can use nonstandard measuring tools such as blocks, paper clips, pumpkins, markers, and so on to measure how tall they are and then compare the heights of the others in the classroom. Children can try arranging the yarn from shortest to tallest and then tallest to shortest. The key point to emphasize is that people are different in many ways and that these differences make life interesting and make us all individuals.

Some Supporting Books

I'm a Pretty Little Black Girl! by Betty Bynum, illustrated by Claire Armstrong Parod

The Colors of Us by Karen Katz

Fine Arts

Free art with human colors. Children can use human-colored paints, crayons, or colored pencils to creatively express themselves. Some children may choose to create people, while others might use the colors to make something entirely different or just to explore the various hues. The idea is to celebrate the beauty of the many shades of colors that make us human.

Some Supporting Books

The Colors of Us by Karen Katz

All the Colors of the Earth by Sheila Hamanaka

Sulwe by Lupita Nyong'o, illustrated by Vashti Harrison

Chalk art. Give each child a black or dark brown piece of paper and chalk and allow children to create whatever design or picture they choose. Because we typically use white or light-colored paper as the background for art, this activity is designed to show that dark colors are useful, normal, and great choices for art.

Some Supporting Books

Black Is a Rainbow Color by Angela Joy

Black Bird Yellow Sun by Steve Light

Tiny art. Give each child an index card, a small paintbrush, and a bit of black paint so they can create tiny black and white masterpieces. Allow the children to paint whatever they want.

Some Supporting Books

Black Is a Rainbow Color by Angela Joy
Black Bird Yellow Sun by Steve Light

Discussion Questions

1. How do you feel about dark skin tones? Light skin tones? How might your views affect the children in your care?
2. What ideas do you have to celebrate all skin tones? To celebrate dark skin tones specifically?
3. Besides the books mentioned, what other child-friendly sources could you use to discuss why we have skin color differences?
4. How are you explicitly celebrating people with dark skin tones?
5. What art activities could you create that focus on dark colors?
6. What changes could you make in your environment to portray darkness and dark skin tones positively?
7. How might the needs of children with two Black biological parents and children with only one Black biological parent differ? What about children with no immediate Black family members?

Talking Black

SUPPORTING MULTILINGUAL CHILDREN

Language develops rapidly during the early childhood years. Most children enter early childhood centers as infants, before they have learned to speak, but by the time they reach kindergarten, typically developing children have near-adult speech. Because of cultural differences that influence speech, we must consider Black children specifically to ensure their language learning experiences are positive.

Children need the opportunity to talk if they are to develop their speaking skills, and classrooms need to have relevant materials and experiences throughout the day that foster these skills. A play-based environment with many opportunities for children to talk, rather than just sitting and listening to the teacher, allows for greater improvement in their speaking skills. Additionally, educators can fill the classroom with materials related to the children's life to facilitate speaking and engagement. When children bring ways of speaking from home, including dialects, languages, mannerisms, style, and volume, that are allowed and celebrated in the classroom, children who have the ability to do so will speak.

In creating games and activities around the sounds in words, including rhyming, syllables, alliteration, and onset and rhyme, we must consider children's interests while also planning for cultural specificity. The same goes for teaching and practicing the names of letters. Teachers can have children make letters themselves with found items and then take pictures of them so that each child can contribute to the design of the classroom. Teachers can also emphasize the names of the children as well as the names of their family members when discussing letters as well as sounds of language. Additionally, teachers can incorporate culturally relevant alphabet books such as *M Is for Melanin: A Celebration of the Black Child* by Tiffany Rose and *A Is for Activist* by Innosanto Nagara.

Having the desire to listen to and engage with books is an important precursor to learning to read. Having access to many different, relevant books encourages this desire. Teachers can explicitly teach print concepts with culturally relevant books, pointing out words, pictures, letters, the direction of the text, punctuation, and other targeted features. Using race-specific books, not just being generally multicultural, conveys how important and significant celebrating racial identity is to the teacher and the goals of the classroom.

Reading areas should feature authentic, diverse books that center on the interests of students, including the Black children. However, there should also be books throughout the classroom so that children who strongly prefer other areas, such as the blocks or the house area, can still self-select books to read. Educators aiming to improve comprehension in their Black students can provide opportunities for students to retell stories in race-specific books. Following up readings with related activities can help increase text comprehension. Additionally, using retelling props often grows children's interest in certain books. Storytelling props for many classic books are available from school supply manufacturers, and teachers can always create their own props for culturally specific books.

From my experience, writing is best when it is authentic rather than forced. Educators can provide blank books in the writing centers of their classrooms and encourage students to write whatever they want. Educators can also implement writing in meaningful ways, such as asking children to sign their names upon arrival and providing paper in the house area to take down orders during restaurant play and in the block area to make signs for structures. Including writing materials as well as books in each area of the classroom helps meet the academic needs of all students regardless of their play preferences. I encourage educators to look at the interests of all students and reflect on how they can infuse authentic writing throughout the day.

Supporting Research

Some Black children speak African American Language (AAL), also known as African American English (AAE), as their first language. While some young AAL speakers are also proficient in Standard American English (SAE), the language of power used in most classrooms in the United States, others will be working to learn SAE upon entering early care and will need support from their teachers as they work toward becoming multilingual. As researchers Margaret Beneke and Gregory A. Cheatham explain, "While African American English (AAE) is one of the most widely recognized English dialects in the United States, the use of AAE in schools and programs has been viewed negatively" (2015, 127). Kamania Wynter-Hoyte and Mukkaramah Smith (2020) take this idea further:

> Anti-Blackness can be recognized in linguistic violence against speakers of AAL. Children who speak AAL in schools are constantly under attack as they are linguistically profiled for speaking the language of comfort, home, family, heritage, and friendship. Despite decades of research that documents AAL as historic, literary, and rule-governed, teachers commit linguicide, or the killing of a language, in classroom spaces because they view AAL as slang, incorrect, or broken English and make judgments about children's intelligence accordingly. (410)

Home Languages Other Than English

It's important to note that some Black children speak a language besides English. Their multilingualism should be fostered as well. Chapter 7 focuses on Black marginalized ethnicities. Teachers who have students in their classroom from those or other ethnic groups should ensure that the home languages of these children are also represented in the classroom through books, displays, and activities.

Gloria Swindler Boutte (2016) argues that educators should consider young speakers of AAL as dual-language learners and nurture the development of both languages, as they are both complex and rule-governed language systems with importance. Early childhood educators should honor the home and community languages of all children, including children who speak AAL. Creating a safe space for language diversity allows children to feel like they belong in the room and can encourage them to speak without the fear of being shunned for speaking another language.

Listening skills are actively developing in the early childhood years. Educators can foster listening skills by engaging in meaningful, multi-turn conversations with children, including their Black children. Additionally, they can provide authentic and culturally relevant books. Research has shown that books portraying Black protagonists engaging in authentically Black behaviors increase young Black children's comprehension (Edwards and Rosin 2016). According to Bell and Clark (1998), when Black children listen to stories with Black protagonists engaging in authentically Black experiences, their recall and comprehension scores are significantly higher than when they hear stories with White protagonists or stories with Black protagonists that engage in Eurocentric activities. Therefore, early childhood educators can target comprehension skills by reading books that have authentic representations of culture and feature characters engaged in activities that mirror the activities of the children and their families. One suggestion for selecting books that authentically portray a group is to select books authored by a member of the group being portrayed. This shared cultural connection between the author and the characters they are creating typically means the story will be authentic.

Real Examples of Good Practice

Supporting multilingual children should include explicitly teaching the differences between the multiple language systems that children are learning while making sure to describe each language form as simply different, not superior to any other form. Boutte (2016) provides a classroom example of this:

> Denise (AAL speaker): Jameka have two balloons.
>
> Teacher: Yes, she does. Do you know how to say that in Standard English?
>
> Denise: Is it, "Jameka has two balloons"?
>
> Teacher: Yes! Wow! You know how to say it two ways! (40)

Educators can also intentionally create experiences that focus on language differences. For example, Beneke and Cheatham (2015) discuss leading a classroom investigation on the different ways people talk and changing how we talk in different situations. Educators and students can explore how some people call items by different names or say the same things using different words in the sentence. It is also worth considering how we change the way we talk in different situations, including code switching or moving between more than one way of speaking to meet the needs of the speaker or listener.

Additionally, early childhood educators can choose children's books that feature AAL in their classrooms for read alouds. Wynter-Hoyte and Smith (2020) include AAL in their own writing and allow the young students to also write in AAL. By legitimizing AAL, allowing it to be used as an acceptable form of language *in addition* to SAE, early childhood educators not only support Black children in their multilingual journeys but also foster their racial identity development, taking out the shame of using a language form that is very much linked to race. Early childhood educators from birth and up can foster children's positive racial identities and increase their confidence by embracing AAL and intentionally selecting texts that authentically portray children's lives.

Practical Solutions for Supporting Multilingual Students

In supporting emerging multilingual students, early childhood educators can include teaching and learning materials in their students' first languages to go along with the many learning materials that are present in the language of instruction. As with the other aspects of racial identity, children's books are an effective means to incorporate the language varieties of the children in the classroom. Teachers can plan to use books that utilize AAL in their read alouds and then use those same books for follow-up activities. By engaging with these books over a length of time, educators transmit the value that they have for AAL. It is also important to include children's books that authentically portray Black people engaged in tasks that would be familiar to the children hearing the story. This familiarity helps emergent readers develop text comprehension skills. Early childhood educators can select books written by Black authors that feature Black characters engaged in culturally specific activities to foster a deeper understanding of literature.

In addition to supporting emerging multilingual children, early childhood educators should also celebrate language diversity in general. Educators can do this with multilingual books that teach young children different ways to say the same thing as well as through planned experiences that are not based on books. By regularly focusing on the idea that people speak and sign in many different ways, educators help to foster an appreciation for language diversity in general. Playing games with language, singing and signing nursery rhymes, and providing opportunities for children to engage in conversations with each other and with adults are all important steps in building future proficient readers.

Given that the focus of this chapter is on language, the sample activities that follow highlight books that foster multilingualism. A twofold approach—celebrating home languages and choosing books with authentic portrayals—is key to celebrating and embracing multilingualism and multiculturalism. In addition to selecting books that achieve these goals, educators can expand on them with hands-on, joyful follow-up experiences. Further, educators can plan experiences that celebrate language diversity in general. The sections that follow illustrate this process.

Supporting Multilingual Infants and Toddlers

Books That Use AAL

Yo! Yes? by Chris Raschka uses very few words on a page to put the reader in the middle of two people who speak a bit differently but are becoming friends. One child speaks AAL while the other speaks SAE. The book is easily read in a highly entertaining way for our littlest learners. Some follow-up activities include:

- *From book to song.* A theatrical version of this book where the text is put into a song can be found via an internet search. Immediately after reading *Yo! Yes?*, later on, or even on a different day, play the theatrical version and then sing the book together.
- *Hello song.* A focus of the book is the difference in the way the two characters speak. To build on this, introduce different ways of saying hello through song. An internet search will find online

recordings of children's songs that teach how to say hello in different languages.

Honey Baby Sugar Child by Alice Faye Duncan, illustrated by Susan Keeter, features a mother who tells her young child how much she loves them, using AAL. The sweet and short read aloud is perfect to engage young learners. Students whose parents speak AAL might see a bit of their home life in the pages. Some follow-up activities include:

- *Sweet taste test.* The mother in *Honey Baby Sugar Child* lovingly compares her baby to sweet things, even commenting that she could eat her baby up. Young children can engage in a sensory activity involving taste, trying small bits of sweet items. Some suggestions are maple syrup, agave nectar, yacon root syrup, coconut nectar, rice syrup, molasses, and honey. Check with families for allergy and dietary concerns in advance. **Note that honey is not safe for children under the age of one.**

- *The Muffin Man.* Staying within the theme of sweets, lead the children in the common nursery rhyme "The Muffin Man." Change the muffin man to the donut man, cupcake man, or other sweet treats to keep the song going longer.

Be Boy Buzz by bell hooks, illustrated by Chris Raschka, is a short board book that follows a young boy who speaks AAL. He uses his language to describe the things he likes about himself and what he can do. Some follow-up activities include:

- *Emotion faces.* The boy talks about the different ways he feels. Young children can connect to the character in the book by exploring their own emotions. Teachers can call out emotions and show pictures of children with those feelings, while the children try to mimic the expressions. Teachers can also talk about things that happen that cause them to feel each emotion.

- *Quiet and loud.* This book also presents a great opportunity to discuss and explore *quiet* and *loud*. Direct students to make loud sounds with their voices, musical instruments, their bodies (clapping), and so on, and then make quiet sounds. Young children will enjoy shifting noise levels in this exploration of opposites.

Books That Authentically Portray Black Lives

The board book *Please, Baby, Please* by Spike Lee and Tonya Lewis Lee, illustrated by Kadir Nelson, follows a young toddler as they make messes, refuse food, and explore their environment as their caregiver begs them to act in a different way. This sweet story authentically portrays the power struggles that arise as older infants and young toddlers start exploring their agency. A similar text is *Please, Puppy, Please* by the same authors and illustrator. A follow-up activity could be taste testing peas together.

Whose Toes Are Those? by Jabari Asim, illustrated by LeUyen Pham, is a sweet board book that features poetic language to describe a young child's feet and toes. The text celebrates the brown skin of the infant or toddler main character while authentically portraying the type of affection children of this age often receive from their caregivers. Follow up the book by taking off shoes and socks and counting toes together. A similar text is *Whose Knees Are These?* by the same author and illustrator.

Count to Love by Andrea Pinkney, illustrated by Brian Pinkney, is a counting board book. In the story, a baby is showered with love and joy as they count. Infants and toddlers alike will interact with the content while seeing the authentic portrayal of Black love and joy, written just for children ages one to three. A similar book is *Counting to Tar Beach* by Faith Ringgold. For a follow-up activity, clap and count once for each number.

The poetic *Baby, Sleepy Baby* by Atinuke, illustrated by Angela Brooksbank, is based on a lullaby the author's father sang to her. Use this book as a read aloud right before naptime. Some other lullaby books are *Lullaby for a Black Mother* by Langston Hughes, illustrated by Sean Qualls, and *Brown*

Baby Lullaby by Tameka Fryer Brown, illustrated by A. G. Ford. In either case, the follow-up activity is simply resting during naptime.

Opportunities to Explore Language Diversity

How Do You Say Hello? class book. Commercially manufactured books work well, but personalized class books are also impactful. To make the *How Do You Say Hello?* class book, educators ask parents to tell them one way that they might greet a close friend or relative that is not hello. The teachers then make a class book featuring pictures of each child with their family's chosen greeting on the opposite page. A small photo album makes a great base for this book.

Popcorn greetings. Parachute games are delightful experiences in early childhood classrooms. Early childhood educators can take soft tissues or paper towels and write different greetings, such as "Hello," "What's Up," "Hola," "'Sup With It?" "Nǐ hǎo," "'Ahlan," "Jambo," and more. The teacher explains that there are lots of different ways to say hello, and then the tissues are balled up and placed on a small parachute or blanket. The educators and children that are able then shake the parachute and watch the white balls of tissue bounce up and down like popcorn. As a tissue falls to the floor, the teacher reads the greeting written on it.

Storytelling. Infant and toddler teachers can invite families who speak different languages (whether it is different varieties of English such as AAL or languages such as Mandarin or Arabic) to come into the classroom to tell a story to the young learners. The children hear the different language varieties used in the stories, which helps normalize the idea of language diversity.

Fostering Multilingualism with Preschoolers

Books That Use AAL

Yesterday I Had the Blues by Jeron Ashford Frame, illustrated by R. Gregory Christie, is both a social-emotional book and a color book. The character uses colors and other metaphors and similes to paint a picture of how he and others feel. Some follow-up activities include:

- *Mono color painting.* The main character describes his and others' moods by using a single color, reflected in the illustrations. Teachers can follow up on this story by allowing children to paint with just one color. Ideally, students are given access to multiple shades of the one color, or black and white paint to mix with their chosen color to create different shades. Invite them to use a word or a sentence to describe their mood, using the color they selected for the painting.
- *Painting to music.* Sticking with the idea of mood and color, allow children to paint to varying music. Encourage the students to paint in the way that the music makes them feel.

Set in the past, *Flossie and the Fox* by Patricia McKissack, illustrated by Rachel Isadora, tells the story of a little girl and a fox. The human characters speak in fluent AAL throughout the entire book, while the fox speaks in SE. This cute story is a bit long, so depending on the children, teachers may choose to read it over more than one story time. Some follow-up activities include the following:

- *Create a fox costume.* The fox in this story is one of the main characters. It's always fun when people and animals talk to each other in stories. Teachers can embrace the fantasy of the fox and play on Flossie's hesitation in believing he really was a fox by guiding children to create their own fox costumes using tape, felt, construction paper, and other art supplies.

- *Reenact the story*. Retelling a story is an important skill for young children. Children can choose the character they want to be (more than one child can be each character) and then work as a class or small group to retell the story, with the help of the teachers as appropriate.

She Come Bringing Me That Little Baby Girl by Eloise Greenfield, illustrated by John Steptoe, is told from the perspective of a new big brother. The story tells of his disappointment with getting a baby sister instead of the baby brother that he requested. He comes around once he realizes that he has a role to play in bringing up his new little sister. Some follow-up activities include the following:

- *Washing and dressing baby dolls*. Children in small groups work on fine-motor skills while at the same time playing pretend and exploring water by washing hard plastic baby dolls with diverse skin tones, using small sponges and towels to wash and dry them. Next, children can practice pulling arms through tiny sleeves, fastening clothes, and other dressing tasks that young children often struggle to complete.
- *Me in the future*. The protagonist was shocked and amused that his uncle and mother were babies once too. Teachers can follow up on the ways that people change as they age by asking their preschoolers to create a self-portrait of what they might look like in the future as a grown-up.

Books That Authentically Portray Black Lives

In the award-winning *The Electric Slide and Kai* by Kelly J. Baptist, illustrated by Darnell Johnson, Kai is learning the Electric Slide, an extremely popular line dance in the African American community, at his aunt's wedding. Many children will have seen their loved ones doing this dance at their own family events. Follow up the book by learning the Electric Slide as a group. A similar book is *I Got the Rhythm* by Connie Schofield-Morrison, illustrated by Frank Morrison.

In *Grandma's Purse* by Vanessa Brantley-Newton, a little girl is excited that her grandmother (whom she calls Mimi) is coming to visit. She is especially excited about the treasures in Mimi's purse. Many children will relate to the joy and mystery of grandmother's purse, along with the joy of receiving a visit from grandma. A potential follow-up activity is making purses out of felt. Educators can fold a large piece of felt in half, punch holes on the sides, and give children large plastic needles and yarn so that the children can "sew" up their purse. A similar book is *Full, Full, Full of Love* by Trish Cooke, illustrated by Paul Howard, which also focuses on a bond between a child and his grandmother.

The child narrator in *My Mommy Medicine* by Edwidge Danticat, illustrated by Shannon Wright, tells how her mommy takes care of her when she is sick. Children will relate to this story about being taken care of by loving caregivers. A fun follow-up activity is pretending to be doctors, nurses, and parents. A similar book is *Leo Gets a Checkup* by Anna McQuinn, illustrated by Ruth Hearson.

Bedtime Bonnet by Nancy Redd, illustrated by Nneka Myers, authentically portrays the nighttime hair care routines of a Black family and how stressful it can be if something does not go just right. The book mentions bonnets, durags, wraps, scarves, and caps. In a follow-up activity, children can author and illustrate their own books about their bedtime routines. A similar book is *Hair Love* by Matthew A. Cherry, illustrated by Vashti Harrison.

Opportunities to Explore Language Diversity

Language investigation. For this activity, preschool teachers tell their students that they are language investigators and that they need to turn on their listening ears to listen for different languages. Then teachers read preselected excerpts from books, switching between reading SAE, AAL, and another language spoken by the children or their families. Children then indicate which language the selected reading uses. Students can celebrate correct answers by clapping, stomping, jumping up and down, or some other active method.

Language collage. Similar to the *How Do You Say Hello?* class book presented in the infant/toddler section, the language collage is a collaborative project. Educators ask families and even children how they greet someone who is a close friend or relative and then write those greetings on butcher paper. After presenting the many different expressions to the students, teachers hand out magazines and art materials for the children to create a language collage together, to be displayed in the classroom or out in the hallway.

Dancing to kids' versions of popular music. Popular music includes many language varieties, including SAE, AAL, Spanish, and, with the growing popularity of K-Pop, Korean. Teachers can capitalize on this variety by playing kids' versions of popular music during music and movement time. By playing music with different languages, educators show the legitimacy of different language forms. As an extension, educators can point out the different language varieties used in songs and even use lyrics that the children know to point out developmentally appropriate language features.

Discussion Questions

1. Before reading this chapter, what were your thoughts on African American Language? Did you know that it was a rule-governed system of language, just as Standard American English is? How might having this knowledge change someone's perspective on the language?
2. Think about your classroom library. Are there books that authentically portray Black characters engaging in activities typical of the group? Are there books that feature speakers of AAL?

3. What supports exist in your setting for multilingual learners who speak languages besides English? Could these supports be offered for children who speak AAL as their first language?
4. Are there speakers of AAL in your setting? How might you support young speakers of AAL? Are there Black children who speak languages besides variations of English in your setting? If so, how are their languages represented?
5. How might allowing multiple forms of language in your classroom contribute to language learning?
6. What parts of your day lend themselves to engaging in meaningful conversations with children?
7. Think about your own identity. What role does language play in defining who you are? How might you feel if you could no longer speak your preferred language variety? How might this influence the way you think about your identity? How might supporting language lead to fostering positive racial identity?

Feeling Good, Feeling Great

SOCIAL-EMOTIONAL CONSIDERATIONS FOR BLACK CHILDREN

Social-emotional development is a paramount consideration in early childhood education. Healthy social-emotional development is a precursor not only for success in school but for life in general. Even though healthy social-emotional development is critical, in many instances it is addressed and planned for only during the early childhood years and given less focus during later school experiences. This oversight makes the work of educators of young children even more critical. Social-emotional development is a broad concept with many components, including self-concept, self-regulation and attention, emotional control, relationships, and social awareness. As we consider social-emotional development in broad terms for all children, however, there are also racial components to contemplate.

Self-concept. It is important that all children develop a sense of pride. This task becomes even more important for Black children, as they are exposed to societal messages that can harm their concept of themselves. Additionally, general approaches that are used to encourage positive self-concepts in other children are also important for Black children, such as having challenging but achievable expectations. Educators must be aware of the expectations they have for each individual child because it is possible to unintentionally have lowered expectations for Black children. These implicitly lowered expectations can lead to Black children feeling less capable than their peers.

Self-regulation and attention. Educators should hold age-appropriate attention expectations for all children. However, as Black children are more likely to get in trouble for misbehavior (Howard 2018), ensuring that attention-intensive tasks are of high interest and related to lived experiences is crucial. One way to do this is to include relevant activities, materials, and discussions in the class. When children are asked to engage in a task that considers their own personal interests and cultural background in an authentic way, they are more engaged.

Emotional control. High-quality early childhood classrooms discuss feelings and emotions with all children. Because Black students deal with typical childhood frustrations along with added stressors related to microaggressions and curious peers, emotions related to race should be discussed specifically, as these can be extremely challenging to handle. For example, children often get frustrated if a peer sits too close to them on the carpet or if another child sits in their square or spot, as young children are still working on spatial recognition and learning about personal space. Black children experience this too, but they, for example, might face an additional challenge of having a peer want to touch their hair. While any child might be teased or left out of a play episode, Black children might be taunted for features central to their identity, like skin color, or be excluded from play because of it. Dealing with scenarios like these is tough, and children may need time to debrief and regroup. One way to do this is to invite children to state their feelings when other children make racially harmful comments. Research has many examples of young children saying racially based hurtful comments and engaging in racially based behaviors (Sturdivant 2021a and 2021b). Effective early childhood educators listen for these instances and step in to teach about race while also soothing the hurt feelings of the child on the receiving end of the harm.

Relationships. As most teachers are White middle-class women, Black children may face a cultural mismatch when entering the classroom, which can negatively affect relationships. Additionally, when a child is a part of a group that is in the minority in the classroom, cultural differences can impede peer relationships. Adults can intentionally incorporate the cultures of all students, especially those in the minority, to prevent certain students from continuously having all of the cultural capital—that is, having their home cultures and the culture of the classroom closely match.

Social awareness. Due to their varied experiences, children from cultural backgrounds outside of the dominant group may have differing opinions and attitudes about what is going on in the class. Educators should intentionally highlight differences in opinions and experiences so children become aware of social differences and so all children feel they belong in the classroom. One way to do this is to ask for different perspectives on situations instead of assuming that all children are excited or sad about the same things. Further, it is also important to acknowledge different perspectives as valid. For example, not all children have the same feelings about community helpers, such as police officers or social workers. Depending on what they have experienced in their community, some helpers may not seem so helpful. These differing perspectives based on their lived realities should be allowed in the classroom, as they are a part of that child's knowledge about the world.

Supporting Research

Young children grapple with and notice race (Sturdivant and Alanís 2019 and 2021). Therefore, they are apt to pick up on differences in the ways that students are treated. There is evidence that early childhood teachers view the actions and emotions of Black children in a far more negative light than their White peers, which could be a factor in the inequitable suspension rates of Black children from early childhood settings (Halberstadt et al. 2020).

Given this inequitable climate in early childhood education, Elizabeth King (2021) calls for anti-oppressive emotion language, starting with toddlers. There are three parts to the anti-oppressive approach to emotions: (1) verbally refer to a child's emotions, (2) validate their feelings, no matter their cultural or racial identity, and (3) counter potential bias by responding in a culturally aware manner. Handling emotions in an anti-oppressive way, actively reflecting on any potential bias in perceptions of children from certain groups, and acknowledging that our cultures inform what we determine is appropriate behavior are necessary steps in culturally responsive classroom management. Culturally relevant classroom management has been shown to be effective in supporting Black children to develop self-regulation (Price and Steed 2016).

Additionally, it is important to acknowledge the emotional experiences of Black children in early childhood classrooms. According to Park (2011), White preschool girls with social power regularly exclude or mistreat their Black peers. Further, young Black children sometimes find themselves in uncomfortable situations due to their non-Black peers' innocent curiosity about their Blackness (Derman-Sparks and Olsen Edwards 2010). In contrast, Glenda MacNaughton, Karina Davis, and Kylie Smith (2010) describe White preschoolers who saw Whiteness as simply normal. This ties into research that finds differences in the ways racial groups talk about emotions (King 2021). In one example, according to Angel D. Dunbar and colleagues (2017), Black families feel a need to emotionally prepare their children for discrimination and bias. This preparation is necessary given the realities of facing racism but also can negatively contribute to a child's developing racial identity.

That young children of different racial groups face these contrasting experiences is sad, but it should also serve as a call for action. It is evidence why social-emotional learning must also consider racial backgrounds, especially if the aim is to foster healthy racial identities.

Real Examples of Good Practice

One culturally responsive approach for supporting healthy social-emotional development and dealing with challenging behaviors is to discuss conflict during group time (Price and Steed 2016). This approach is a great way to tackle harmful racial comments made by children. By discussing those situations in a group, all children can learn why certain comments are harmful and how they make their peers feel, which could prevent additional future harm. Further, children who have experienced harmful behaviors from their peers that were not witnessed by an adult can also regain some confidence through the discussions. By taking harmful racial comments and behaviors seriously, early childhood educators show their support and commitment to their Black students, creating a safe learning community.

Another approach is to read books on social-emotional topics out loud. Shauna Tominey and colleagues (2017) suggest that early childhood educators can use books to introduce new feelings vocabulary words and make photocopies of pages to post around the room as examples of feelings. These pages can help young children identify and state their feelings during challenging moments. In addition to teaching vocabulary, books that touch on stressors due to race also validate feelings that children may be having and provide them with the opportunity to discuss their experiences. Examples of books like this are detailed in the practical solutions section.

A final approach to support healthy social-emotional development is making sure that Black children feel seen throughout the curriculum. Brian L. Wright (2019) discusses using history to affirm identities through a "history and me" project, which intentionally presents important historical figures who match the social identities of the children in the class. This can help Black children feel a sense of pride in their racial group and foster confidence and self-esteem. Vashti Harrison's Little Leaders books, discussed in chapter 3, can serve as starting points for early childhood identity-affirming history lessons.

Practical Solutions to Support Social-Emotional Development

Self-Concept

Simple actions from educators to bolster children's self-concept can go a long way. In addition to holding high expectations for children, educators should allow for student choice. Educators can consider teaching children to do everyday tasks on their own, like putting on their jackets and opening food items, to foster self-confidence, keeping in mind cultural notions about what is appropriate for a child to do for themselves. Educators can also take care to acknowledge the efforts of all their students and make sure that the Black children are not being unintentionally overlooked. A common activity in early childhood classrooms is sending home an All About Me page at the beginning of the year. To foster a sense of pride in Black children, educators can add to this activity by celebrating differences that are often silenced, such as hair texture and skin, hair, and eye color. Just as we celebrate children for their favorite colors, foods, and pets, we can also celebrate children for the names they give to the color of their skin and the texture of their hair. This addition is important for Black children because they are less likely to feel that their skin color and hair texture are celebrated outside of their home. By including these personal aspects, educators can show children that they are important and special enough to talk about and that these aspects are positive attributes.

Self-Regulation and Attention

Infant and toddler teachers can target self-regulation and attention through copying games in which young children mimic the facial expressions of their teachers. Teachers provide commentary to go along with their emotions (for example, *I'm feeling so happy, my mommy put puffs in my hair* or *I'm feeling sad because someone said something mean about my hair*). Preschool educators can use cultural cues for transitions during and in between activities, such as call-and-response techniques that hold the children's attention and highlight student interests. The teacher says an agreed-upon word or phrase to get the class's attention, and then the students reply with a separate agreed-upon word or phrase. Using cultural references for the call-and-response can make the cognitive task of having to stop working on an activity and attend to something else more appealing for children, making the transition easier and leading to better self-regulation.

Emotional Control

Controlling emotions is one of the major skills young children work to achieve in early childhood classrooms. Many early childhood classrooms have areas in the classroom dedicated to feelings—sometimes with a feelings chart or with dolls that represent different emotions. When adults hear a child make a racially harmful comment, they can help the Black child gain some power back by allowing them to state the way they feel and to also ensure that the other child understands that their language was hurtful. Educators do not have to wait for incidents to occur to talk about emotions and race-related experiences, and any time they discuss emotions with the class they can include hypothetical situations related to race. For instance, they can talk about how someone might feel after getting new braids (proud?) or being asked why their skin is so dark (sad, confused?). The hypothetical examples we use to discuss emotions should not be color-blind. Additionally, some teachers use puppets to tell stories about feelings. Using racially diverse puppets helps scenarios related to racial appearance seem more organic.

Relationships

Teachers can foster adult-child relationships by including culturally specific greetings, like popular dances, handshakes, and gestures from movies or television shows, and by singing culturally responsive songs, nursery rhymes, and chants. Relationships blossom when adults talk to children at their eye level about topics the students are interested in (Sturdivant and Alanís 2019).

Educators can nurture relationships among peers by explicitly teaching conflict resolution skills. It is inevitable that children have conflicts, but when children are empowered to resolve them, they can advocate for themselves without being aggressive. Preschool educators can provide enough classroom jobs for everyone in the class to prevent bias and disengagement and then allow the children to select their own jobs. They also can rotate the students who work together in small groups so that children spend time with a variety of others.

Social Awareness

Early childhood educators can use socially aware children's books to offer different perspectives about what is going on in the world and lead conversations that might cause children to think differently or validate their developing beliefs about the world. Infant and toddler teachers can read books like *Who? A Celebration of Babies* by Robie H. Harris, *Woke Baby* by Mahogany L. Browne, *Antiracist Baby* by Ibram X. Kendi, *A Little Book about Justice* by Ashwin Chacko, *A Little Book about Racism* by Jelani Memory, and *A Little Book about Activism* by Courtney Ahn.

In addition to the books mentioned here, preschool teachers can introduce books like *A Is for Activist* and *Counting on Community* by Innosanto Nagara, *Together* by Mona Damluji, *An ABC of Equality* by Chana Ginelle Ewing, *A Kids Book about Racism* by Jelani Memory, *A Kids Book about Diversity* by Charnaie Gordon, *A Kids Book about Systemic Racism* by Jordan Thierry, and *Change Sings: A Children's Anthem* by Amanda Gorman.

In general, being a part of a racial group that is very often framed in a negative light from a variety of sources can be stressful. By considering this fact in the development of social-emotional experiences for young children, educators can help to foster resilience within a group that will need to be resilient to be successful in life. In addition to the activities and books mentioned previously, educators can analyze what they are already doing to support social-emotional learning and think about how to move those practices from being silent about race to being informed by our racialized environment. Educators can look at the books, puppets, and other tools, like posters and safe areas or cozy corners, to examine if race or culture is mentioned or considered. If race is absent, teachers can reflect on the racial components of social-emotional learning put forward in this chapter and plan to incorporate the new information where appropriate.

Discussion Questions

1. On the spectrum of seeing yourself as "normal"—as defined by the White preschoolers mentioned in this chapter's research section—to facing racial microaggressions to experiencing open hostility, what has your experience with race been? How might those experiences have influenced your social-emotional development?
2. Think of the children in your care and their families. What might their experiences with race have been, and how might those experiences affect the children's social-emotional development?
3. How comfortable do you currently feel talking about racial situations and emotions with young children? If you are uncomfortable, how could you increase your comfort level?

4. What do you currently do to support the social-emotional development of the children in your care? What changes or additions could you make to include race in your social-emotional program?
5. How might non-Black students benefit from racially aware social-emotional development?
6. How might partnering with families help support racially aware social-emotional learning?
7. What tangible materials might you need to add to your classroom to facilitate racially aware social-emotional development?

Representation Matters

CENTERING BLACK CHARACTERS IN CHILDREN'S LITERATURE

The characters the children watched on televisions, phones, and tablets were a frequent topic of conversation in the classroom in which I conducted my study. The children also talked about dressing up as certain characters and pretended to talk on the phone to various characters, go to their houses, and meet them at shops, and the students often sang their shows' theme songs together. These children characters played a major role in the lives of these preschoolers. Unfortunately, the only characters that were talked about and celebrated by the students that I witnessed were White. With a limited quantity of Black characters in children's digital media and even fewer Black characters who are given interesting and exciting lives, it is not shocking that the children did not talk much about Black characters. Further, given the prevalence of anti-Blackness as discussed in previous chapters, it will take a sustained and consistent effort of celebrating Blackness and Black characters to cancel out the prevailing view of Blackness as undesirable.

By intentionally exposing young children to interesting and exciting Black characters, early childhood educators can help to foster positive identities. Additionally, educators can work to include characters with multiracial backgrounds to offer support for bi- and multiracial Black children. In showing the diversity of Black families, early childhood educators can ensure that their Black children are not seen as a monolith or a single type of people but as a diverse group with varying experiences. The power of representation is that it helps people to feel seen and to know that their experiences are valid and worthy of being celebrated. This feeling is powerful because it also sends the message that they themselves are worthy—and this is the goal of fostering positive racial identity.

Supporting Research

Despite BI&POC children making up more than 50 percent of the US population, the majority of leading children's animated characters are White, non-Hispanic males (Hamlen and Imbesi 2020). This is significant because research has found that media have an impact on children's attitudes about race specifically (Winkler 2012). Many of the popular children's movies are based on fairy tales, such as the Grimm brothers' fairy tales (Triska 2017). According to Ann Schmiesing (2016), *The Grimm's Children's and Household Tales (Kinder-und Hausmärchen)* use the color black to represent a variety of negative concepts, including punishment, the devil or demonic forces, menial tasks, and curses. While these original classic tales are uncommonly read today, their variations and themes live on in present-day children's movies and media. Unfortunately, this negative connotation for Blackness is still woven into many celebrated children's stories and movies, including some of the most popular children's movies of all time (Breaux 2010) such as Disney's *Cinderella*, *Snow White*, and *Tangled* (Rapunzel).

In looking at the messages and representation in advertisements, researchers have found that although there has been an increase in the number of Black people featured in advertisements over time, Black people are still far more likely to play unimportant characters and are still portrayed in stereotypical ways (Davis 2018). In addition, Gholnecsar Muhammad and Sherell McArthur (2015) found that the Black girls in their study often discussed the media's portrayal of natural African hair as being undesirable, adding weight to the argument that children notice the messages found within media and grapple with them.

Research has also been conducted on children's television programs, and findings show that 65 percent of characters were White, children of color were far more likely to be girls than boys, and all girls were more likely to be thin than heavy (Lemish and Johnson 2019). Despite parents' best intentions, unfavorable media portrayals in conjunction with other social factors contribute to a child's racial learning and can negatively influence their identity development.

Real Examples of Good Practice

Despite the issues with representation and portrayal in children's media, media remains a powerful tool to boost the confidence of children. For example, Shanna Kohn and colleagues (2020) discuss the power of Arabic-language *Sesame Street* in helping heal young Syrian children emotionally after being traumatized from the conflict in their homeland. Further, Chip Donohue and Roberta Schomburg (2017) call for mentorship around media, with adults talking the young children through what they see and hear. This approach could help in countering so many of the negative messages that researchers have found in examining children's media. Speaking out against negative portrayals or the erasure of groups in media is also empowering, as it teaches children that they are not limited to what others have created and that their thoughts about the world matter.

While educators have little control over how the digital media portrays children and people who share their racial and ethnic characteristics, teachers do have control over what media they share with their class. Picture books are a powerful form of media, and early childhood educators can harness that power to represent the backgrounds of their students. As Shannon B. Wanless and Patricia A. Crawford (2016, 11) argue, "Children need access to books that reflect their own race, culture, experiences, and context. Literature should include representations of different aspects of daily life within a culture, with particular attention given to aspects of setting and racial relevance." Early childhood educators can and do support the developing racial identities of their students by reading and making picture books available that authentically portray the lived experiences of the children in their care.

Practical Solutions for Providing Positive Representations

Early childhood educators can read storybooks with Black main characters living authentic Black lives, not only to validate the experiences of their Black students but also to give their students characters similar to them whom they can pretend to be and talk about during their play. High-quality picture books can leave a lasting impression, just as television shows and movies do. When we come back to the same books or the same characters in different books, over and over again, we create a universe in the minds of the children. These imagined worlds include these characters who represent who children are. Simply reading high-quality books with young children in an engaging way, taking care to make connections and to engage in age-appropriate chats about the stories, is a valuable part of promoting positive racial identity. However, if desired, early childhood educators can also plan experiences to extend the books into hands-on activities. How books are extended can depend on the needs of the children in the classroom.

In the following sections, I discuss children's books that lend themselves to meaningful and interactive reading experiences that are appropriate for infants, toddlers, and preschoolers. These books do not represent an exhaustive list of what can be read aloud in an early childhood class but are simply some suggestions that are generally easy to purchase or check out at a local library. The key in selecting books for representation is to think about whether the plot of the book is relatable and whether a child would want to emulate the protagonist in some way.

A Baby Like Me

The character Leo is a Black baby boy and a little brother. A series of books written by Anna McQuinn and illustrated by Ruth Hearson tells all about his life. By exploring Leo's world over and over by rereading all the stories, children can feel immersed in his life, similar to our adult experience with watching digital media, while feeling valued as they recognize the similarities between his life and theirs.

- *Leo Loves Baby Time*
- *Leo Can Swim*
- *Leo Gets a Checkup*
- *Leo Loves Mommy*
- *Leo Loves Daddy*

Infant teachers can also read aloud books that portray Black children simply living their everyday lives. These stories, meant to entertain, also serve as a reminder that Black lives and experiences are a normal and valid part of human experiences.

- *Every Little Thing* adapted by Cedella Marley, illustrated by Vanessa Brantley-Newton
- *F Is for Feelings* by Goldie Millar and Lisa A. Berger
- *Joshua by the Sea* by Angela Johnson, illustrated by Rhonda Mitchell
- *Little You* by Richard Van Camp, illustrated by Julie Flett
- *Peekaboo Morning* by Rachel Isadora

In addition to book series and storybooks focused on Black children, in general, consider the representation of biracial Black children specifically because their families can look very different from monoracial Black children.

- *A Welcome Song for Baby* by Marsha Diane Arnold
- *Where's Lenny?* by Ken Wilson-Max
- *Let's Feed the Ducks* by Pamela Venus
- *Oscar's Half Birthday* by Bob Graham
- *Ten Tiny Tickles* by Karen Katz
- *"More More More," Said the Baby* by Vera B. Williams

To bolster the read alouds, infant teachers can also display pictures of the children in the class and their families around the room alongside artwork of the characters from these books. By representing the children in the class through photographs and through characters similar to them, infant teachers help create an environment in which children are celebrated for being exactly who they are.

A Toddler Like Me

Toddler teachers can use any of the books mentioned in the infant section with the children in their care. Short books about family and babies are very much of interest to toddlers as well. As toddlers' attention spans increase, teachers can take the opportunity to share slightly longer stories and stories with toddler-age characters the children can identify with.

The character Lola is the older sister of Leo, who is mentioned in the infant section. The adorable stories about this young Black girl are relatable and positive. Her realistic life and experiences with her parents help children connect with her. The Lola books are written by Anna McQuinn and illustrated by Rosalind Beardshaw and are available in English and Spanish.

- *Lola at the Library*
- *Lola Loves Stories*
- *Lola Sleeps Over*
- *Lola Reads to Leo*
- *Lola Gets a Cat*
- *Lola Goes to School*
- *Lola Plants a Garden*
- *Lola at the Library*

As recommended for infants, displaying artwork of Lola and other characters in the classroom can remind the children of the character even when the books are not being read aloud. Toddler teachers can also expand these stories into interactive experiences by having children role-play the different family members in the stories, to the best of their abilities.

Stories that feature Black toddlers and young preschoolers as they are going about their lives and experiencing the love and joy of their families help Black children feel seen and validated.

- *All the World* by Liz Garton
- *Daddy Calls Me Man* by Angela Johnson, illustrated by Rhonda Mitchell
- *Feast for 10* by Cathryn Falwell
- *Full, Full, Full of Love* by Trish Cooke
- *Girl of Mine* by Jabari Asim, illustrated by LeUyen Pham
- *My Aunt Came Back* by Pat Cummings
- *Nana's Cold Days* by Adwoa Badoe, illustrated by Bushra Juniad
- *One Love* adapted by Cedella Marley, illustrated by Vanessa Brantley-Newton

Educators can select specific resources to support the racial identities of biracial Black toddlers. Toddlers, especially older ones, are working on matching and may have questions about how a child "matches" the caregivers who bring them to and from class. Biracial toddlers may also be forming questions about how and why their families and those of their peers differ. By reading books that feature biracial toddlers, early childhood educators help normalize their experiences and demystify some reasons why family members might look different from one another, in terms of race.

- *The Hello Goodbye Window* by Norton Juster, illustrated by Chris Raschka
- *15 Things Not to Do with a Baby* by Margaret McAllister, illustrated by Holly Sterling
- *Henry Wants More* by Linda Ashman, illustrated by Brooke Boynton Hughes
- *Cinnamon Baby* by Nicola Winstanley

Tying the books to some sort of dramatic play is a great extension activity. Consider whether the books lend themselves to adding new materials to the dramatic play center, if there are parts of the books that could be acted out together, or if the book presents a world so interesting that the dramatic play center could be transformed into the setting of the book. Toddler teachers can also consider art extension activities. What aspects of the illustrations stand out that could inspire art? Could the children paint with similar colors? The goal after the read alouds is not necessarily to engage in an activity that is focused on race but rather to keep the children thinking about the book even after the read aloud has ended.

A Kid Like Me

Any of the books mentioned in the infant or toddler sections could also be read to preschoolers or made available in a preschool classroom. The following sections present books and examples of extension activities. All children benefit from simply being read to and engaging with books, but as children get older, many teachers desire to or must also connect reading experiences to activities. This section keeps that in mind.

Books by Keats. Ezra Jack Keats created stories around friends who lived in one neighborhood. The stories often feature a Black boy as the protagonist, and Black students will feel represented because of the characters. Additionally, because the stories take place in an urban environment in multifamily housing, children who hardly ever see their living environments reflected in children's books get to see people who live in similar ways. *A Snowy Day*, Keats's most famous book, has also been adapted into an animated movie. Sharing the book and the movie with preschoolers further engages them.

- *Goggles!*
- *Hi, Cat!*
- *Keats's Neighborhood*
- *A Letter to Amy*
- *Pet Show!*
- *Peter's Chair*
- *The Snowy Day*
- *The Trip*
- *Whistle for Willie*

To connect with these books, invite children to create new stories featuring the characters in Keats's work. Preschoolers can "write" or discuss what they know about the different characters after reading the many books featuring them. Or they can work together to create a cast of original characters as a class and write their own stories with those characters. In the end, teachers can collect the stories in a classroom library filled with characters from the imagined neighborhood of the children in the class. These same extension activities can be done with any series of books.

Ada Twist, Scientist by Andrea Beaty, illustrated by David Roberts, follows a young and highly intelligent Black girl as she embarks on a scientific journey to figure out what is smelling so badly. We see the challenges she faces for having the mind of a scientist as well as the steps her family takes to better support her. The book is lengthy, so it would likely need to be read over more than one day. Additionally, this book, along with similar books from the same author, has been adapted into an animated show by the same name.

- *Measurement: How many cups?* Each child in a small group needs a small cup and a plastic beaker or graduated cylinder and something to document their findings (such as paper and pencil). The children count how many cups of water it takes to fill up the beaker or graduated cylinder and write down their answers. Students can share one large container of water placed in the middle of the table, or you can fill a sand and water table with water so a small group of children can work on all sides of it. Extend the activity by giving each child a different size of container, or provide various sizes of cups so children can compare the differing amounts it takes to fill up the same container.

- *Physical science: Guess the smell.* Provide children with something to cover their eyes, such as a blindfold, and invite them to try to guess a smell placed under their nose. Alternatively, place something within a sensory box that children cannot see inside and have them guess what it is by smell.

Peeny Butter Fudge by Toni Morrison and Slade Morrison, illustrated by Joe Cepeda, tells the story of young children having fun with their grandmother while their parent is away. Together they work on a puzzle and make peanut butter fudge.

- *Geometry: Floor puzzle.* As a whole or a small group, students work together to complete a large floor puzzle. Ensure there are enough puzzle pieces for each child to be able to place at least one piece into the puzzle.

- *Physical science: Lemonade recipe.* For this activity, each child needs access to a large cup of water, some lemon juice or lemons, and sugar or honey. In addition, each child needs an empty cup, a spoon, a writing utensil, and a blank recipe card. Children use the materials to make their perfect glass of lemonade and write down their recipe to share with their peers.

Just Like Josh Gibson by Angela Johnson, illustrated by Beth Peck, talks about how the intersections of race and gender can be a troubling space for a woman athlete and how this was especially true in the past. This is a story of a grandmother who was incredibly talented in baseball but faced limits due to aspects of herself that had nothing to do with her athletic ability.

- *Arithmetic: Sports stories.* Children use sports-related math manipulatives to solve addition and subtraction stories. Educators can make up stories related to the sports-themed manipulatives that are already available in the classroom. For example, if there is a set of sports balls counters, give each child a set of ten counters and say something like, "There were five balls on the field, and then the player kicked two balls off. How many balls are left on the field?"

- *Physical science: What ball goes the farthest?* This activity requires a variety of balls. Students make and write down predictions about which ball they will be able to kick, throw, and or roll the farthest. This science exploration is designed to be done outside. After all the predictions are tested, students can write down the results and share their explanations for what happened.

The rhythmic book *I Got the Rhythm* by Connie Schofield-Morrison, illustrated by Frank Morrison, features a carefree Black girl who hears the rhythm in the everyday activities in her neighborhood. This is a quick read with plenty of opportunities for educators to incorporate movement.

- *Classification and patterning: Clapping patterns.* Students and teachers can clap together in patterns. Perhaps the class starts with clapping up high and then clapping down low and then repeating, to clap out an AB pattern. Or perhaps the class claps behind their backs, under their legs, and then to the side to make an ABC clapping pattern. Children will come up with even more fun and interesting ways to clap and repeat to make a pattern.

- *Life science: Naming body parts.* To begin, play a simple game of head, shoulders, knees, and toes. To make the game more interesting, teachers can lead the interactive song several times but at different speeds. The fast version is always a favorite! After the melody of the song is quite familiar, educators and children can work together to change the lyrics to different body parts. Naming parts of our body like forearms, shins, and heels introduces children to new vocabulary words. Like the original version, the new song the class creates can then be sung at different speeds.

Biracial children may experience microaggressions uniquely related to having parents who are not the same race. Black children who have been adopted by parents of a different race will also benefit from seeing multiracial families represented. In either instance, these children may be confused about their own identity and find it difficult to respond to questions from their peers. They may also find it difficult to figure out where their place is in a very racialized society. Children's books that celebrate families of more than one race and feature children like them will help their self-confidence and potentially give them characters similar to themselves to admire.

Black Is Brown Is Tan by Arnold Adoff, illustrated by Emily Arnold McCully, is a poetic book about a family with a Black mom and a White father. We see a bit of what happens in the lives of the family. We also hear skin tones compared to milk, chocolate, and chocolate milk and hear about children getting bigger and bigger. Educators can extend this book with activities that focus on those things.

- *Physical science: Chocolate milk recipes.* Similar to the lemonade recipe from page 75, students can use milk (or milk substitutes) and chocolate syrup to make their very own recipes for the best cup of chocolate milk.

A Note about Skin Tones and Food

It is important to note that some BI&POC families have expressed displeasure at having their skin compared to food, as this comparison can feel objectifying. I include *Black Is Brown Is Tan* because all family members, including the white father, have their skin compared to food. However, educators may find it valuable to have a conversation with families to understand their comfort level with this comparison before engaging in this or a similar activity.

Mixed Me! by Taye Diggs, illustrated by Shane W. Evans, tells the story of Mike, who has a Black father and a White mother. Mike faces microaggressions from peers who wonder why his parents are not the same race. The story is a declaration of pride in who he is, despite the negativity he faces.

- *Creative self-expression: Describing me.* Invite children to create a self-portrait of themselves doing something they love to do. When they have completed their portraits, ask them to choose one word to describe themselves and write it on their artwork (with adult assistance as needed).

Honeysmoke: A Story of Finding Your Color by Monique Fields, illustrated by Yesenia Moises, follows a young girl, Simone, who has a Black mother and a White father. She asks her parents and peers what color she is and gets mixed responses. She spends some time interacting with her environment and thinking about her color. She eventually creates her own color for herself: honeysmoke. The book ends with a challenge for readers to discover their own color words.

- *Creative self-expression: Discover your color word.* Give children child-safe mirrors and paint swatches to examine their skin. Children then spend time thinking about the word they would use to describe their color. To finish, children make mini presentations to tell classmates about the word they have chosen.

My Two Grannies by Floella Benjamin, illustrated by Margaret Chamberlain, is about Alvina, a girl with one grandmother from the Caribbean and another from Britain. Alvina loves to hear the stories about her grandmothers' homelands, listen to music, and spend quality time with them both despite the women's very different experiences and preferences.

- *Responding to music: Cultural music.* Ask families the names of songs they listen to in their homes. After compiling the responses, make a playlist with some of the songs. During large-group time, the class can dance to the different music. Children will be pleasantly surprised to hear music from their homes played at school.

The Airport Book by Lisa Brown features a family with a Black father and a White mother who are taking a trip via an airplane. The book does not focus on the family as much as the act of taking a trip via an airplane and the procedures to take such a trip.

- *Dramatic expression: Flight simulation.* Teachers and students can pretend to take an airplane ride to a destination. Arrange the chairs in the classroom in rows. Children can use art materials to make airplane boarding passes and use backpacks to represent luggage. Then they can take turns pretending to be the pilot and copilot, flight attendants, and passengers. If a projector is available, the teacher can display clouds on the screen to make the experience even more realistic. Alternatively, prior to the lesson, teachers can take a large sheet of paper outside and invite children to draw what they see in the sky. Another option is to show children images of Earth from the point of view of a plane passenger looking out the window and invite children to draw their versions. Either of these class illustrations can add realism during the flight simulation.

Discussion Questions

1. Which characters do many of your students talk about? Do these characters look like them? What is it about those characters that seems appealing?
2. Which characters can you introduce to your class that have a similar appeal as the ones that they are already interested in exploring? Do they really like superheroes? Princesses? Astronauts?
3. What picture book series that feature Black protagonists are available at your local public library? If none, how could you go about requesting that the library purchase some of the series featured in this chapter or others?
4. Who are Black people within your community who could be invited into the classroom to help your Black students feel confident?
5. What ongoing project could you plan related to a character or characters from a book?
6. Besides children's books, what are some other ways you could represent your Black children in your classroom?
7. In what ways could you involve families in your practice of representing your students?

All Black Lives

CONSIDERING THE MULTIPLE IDENTITIES OF BLACK CHILDREN

Up until this point, this book has covered concepts specific to race. Being Black in an anti-Black society is a challenge, and therefore race should be considered specifically. However, Black children are not a monolith. Each person has many different social identities; race is just one of them. Overall, the individual's combination of social identities and the level of importance of each identity relative to the others give each person a unique cultural profile. Therefore, in trying to foster positive identities in Black children, effective educators should also include positive representations of the intersections of race and children's other marginalized social identities. Some examples of social identities beyond race include ethnicity, religion, disability, gender, sexuality, and class. Some social identities are both celebrated and normalized in our greater society. Others are clearly not celebrated, other than by the people who themselves hold those identities, and are regularly portrayed in a negative light or not portrayed at all.

These connected identities make us who we are and shape the way we experience the world. For example, there was a difference in the play of the Black girls and the Black boys in the classroom I studied. The girls, as targets of advertising and ideals about Eurocentric feminine beauty standards, integrated their attitudes about the worth of the dolls in the way they also changed themselves in play. The boys showed an internalization of anti-Black ideals by the way that they played with the Black dolls. However, I did not observe the boys moving from mistreating the Black dolls to overtly desiring to change a part of themselves as I saw with the girls. This difference in the way we socialize people of different genders played a role in the difference between behaviors that I saw.

When thinking about children's multiple identities, we must intentionally plan for those that are marginalized, as they are the identities that are more likely to be left out in adopted curricula or other selected materials. When educators are intentional about planning to counter societal messaging by celebrating and normalizing what was not considered "normal" or celebrated before, we better support children in developing into confident and healthy versions of themselves.

Supporting Research

In thinking about the experience of Black women, Kimberlé Crenshaw (1989) discusses intersectionality as the experience of being marginalized as a woman while at the same time being marginalized as a Black person. According to Crenshaw (1992), when anti-racist work does not counter male domination or when feminist work does not address racism, neither adequately meets the needs of Black women. This idea of intersectionality can be applied to other ills of society. Combining anti-Blackness with xenophobia (discrimination against perceived immigrants), ableism (discrimination against disabled people), and other structural forms of inequity and discrimination paints a more specific picture about what messages children are internalizing that may harm their developing racial identities.

For example, being Black and disabled leads to different experiences than being Black without a disability. Black people living in poverty have different experiences than Black middle-class people. While Black people within these groups share experiences around race, the differences in their experiences are also significant. Because young children (and even adults) are not necessarily able to separate the way they experience the world through their different identities, we must consider more than race, especially because our society tends to multiply marginalization, and Black people experience marginalization for the color of their skin that intensifies as marginalized identities are added. While all people who fall within marginalized categories may not be able to articulate specific ways that they have faced discrimination, when they realize they are receiving different treatment, they pick up on others' deficit views related to their identities. For example, when a visitor entered my classroom, walked past me, and addressed her question to the instructional assistant, I was not sure if she assumed the instructional assistant was the teacher of record because she was slightly older than me or because she was not Black.

With a focus on early childhood education specifically, Mariana Souto-Manning and Ayesha Rabadi-Raol (2018) argue that high-quality early childhood education must see the multiple marginalized identities of young children as assets and as sources of information that influence our practices. Ryan F. Lei and Marjorie Rhodes (2021) argue that because child development research has focused on one social category at a time, we have information about children's feelings about race, for example, but need more information about how those feelings differ when considering other marginalized social identities combined with race. The idea is that if we acknowledge that other forms of human diversity also come with oppression and inequitable experiences, then we must consider those identities as well, one example being disability. According to Hailey R. Love and Margaret R. Beneke (2021, 37), "once labeled as disabled, Black and Latinx children are disproportionately placed in segregated settings compared to white children with dis/abilities, regardless of family income."

Black children with multiple marginalized identities experience the world through their identities, and these identities have real consequences for their lived experiences. Because of these often negative consequences, caused by deficit views and inequitable power structures, we as early childhood educators should intentionally consider ways to celebrate children who are marginalized in multiple ways. When we take care to intentionally celebrate identities that are ignored at best or overtly criticized at worst, we help facilitate confidence and pride in children's whole selves.

Practical Solutions

To support children's multiple marginalized identities, educators must first reflect honestly about which identities are marginalized in our society. Educators must accept this reality and make a commitment to consciously focus on demographic types that are considered outside of the "norm" and not privileged. As when considering race alone, a great entry point in this form of resistance is via children's books. Simply engaging in an interactive read aloud in which identities that are hidden from the mainstream take center stage is quite helpful. Sharing engaging stories and asking students to participate at their age and ability level is key. Tying stories to engaging, follow-up activities extends the celebration beyond the time spent reading the story.

Additionally, educators must have information about the identities of the families so they can create activities that tap into the multiple identities of the children in their care. Sending home a questionnaire with new families can give educators a place from which to start planning. Given the nature of the questions, it is important to share with families why you are seeking the information so that they feel safe. Reassure parents that you simply want to reflect the diversity of the classroom as you are planning lessons so that each child feels represented and valued. However, it is also important to not pressure families to share anything that they do not feel comfortable sharing. Respect is key.

After identifying the multiple identities of the families, through conversations, questionnaires, or observations, early childhood educators can search for materials that attend to the various identities of the children.

Educators can then think about the activities their children enjoy and how they can combine the content of the books with favorite activities. The process of combining the content of a book with an activity can be challenging at the beginning but will become easier with time. To illustrate this process, children's books that highlight various identities in combination with being Black are listed along with follow-up experiences. The books serve as examples, and the list is not meant to be exhaustive of all of the texts on each subject but instead can be used as support for a continued journey beyond this book.

Being Black and a Member of a Marginalized Ethnicity

For many people in the United States, Blackness is synonymous with the descendants of enslaved Africans who were forced to work here for hundreds of years. This group, of which I am a part, has faced and continues to face oppressive practices and identity-harming messaging. This continued state of harm necessitates practices that honor our identity. African Americans, though, are not the only group of Black people that exist within the United States nor the only group that is marginalized. Different Black ethnic groups, including groups from the Caribbean, Latin America, and parts of Africa, also endure negative experiences and portrayals. While it can be visually obvious when a person is Black, whether someone is a member of a specific ethnic group is likely less so. Educators must get to know who the children and the families that they serve are to ensure that they have a full picture of their racial and ethnic identities.

Infant and Toddlers

Latinx. One way to support children from marginalized ethnicities is to read books in their home language that feature characters that look like them. One example is the Spanish and English book *Rest & Relax / Descansa Y Relájate* by

Whitney Stewart, illustrated by Rocío Alejandro. Another example is *Brown Baby Lullaby* by Tameka Fryer Brown, which is written in English with Spanish words throughout. Infant and toddler teachers can quietly read these books before a nap, encouraging the young child to rest and relax. Infant and toddler teachers can also look for other books, appropriate for the age of the children, that are dually focused on race and ethnicity by displaying characters of a certain race and featuring a language related to that ethnicity.

Africa and the Caribbean. Infant and toddler teachers can also support marginalized ethnicities by sharing fun books that portray a way of life more common in some geographic regions than others. An example of this is *Baby Goes to Market* by Atinuke, illustrated by Angela Brooksbank. In this story, a baby goes to an open-air market with his mother. While there, they get a bit of food from several merchants without their mother knowing, as they are comfortable on their mother's back in a West African–print baby-carrying wrap. The book is funny and cute and will connect with Black children who are from places where open-air markets are common, such as West Africa, or who have family members from these places. Because the baby tried different foods from the different merchants, as an extension activity infants and toddlers could also try some of the foods mentioned in the book, such as bananas, corn, and coconut, keeping allergies and currently introduced foods in mind.

Preschoolers

Preschool teachers can acknowledge Afro-Latinx people by intentionally reading books that celebrate this identity. Caribbean ethnicities are also dually marginalized Black identities. Afro-Latinx people are often erased—intentionally or not—from media about Latinx peoples. *Islandborn* by Junot Díaz, illustrated by Leo Espinosa; *If Dominican Were a Color* by Sili Recio, illustrated by Brianna McCarthy; and *Kitchen Dance*, written and illustrated by Maurie J. Manning, are three beautifully illustrated, engaging children's books that focus on Black Latinx people. *Islandborn* and *If Dominican Were a Color*, both centered on the Dominican Republic, mention the ocean, so a follow-up activity could include exploring a sand and water table filled with ocean animals. A follow-up activity for *Kitchen Dance* could be a class dance party, possibly even a pajama dance party!

Preschool teachers can celebrate Haitian identity by reading a book such as *Calling the Water Drum* by LaTisha Redding, illustrated by Aaron Boyd, then guiding students to explore sound by making drums or other musical instruments out of household products. Preschool teachers can support the developing identities of Trinidadian students by reading a story like *Kamal Goes to Trinidad* by Malcolm Frederick, illustrated by Prodeepta Das, and then engaging in a music and movement activity using calypso music. The book *Malaika's Costume* by Nadia L. Hohn, illustrated by Irene Luxbacher, tells the story of a young Caribbean girl celebrating Carnival for the first time without her mother, who is in Canada to work and send money to her family. Students can "sew" their own costumes using felt, large plastic needles, and yarn, or teachers can make butcher-paper smocks for each child to decorate with art materials to create a costume.

The continent of Africa is an extremely diverse land with more than two thousand languages spoken and more than three thousand distinct ethnicities. Additionally, there is a great difference in the lives of African people, depending on the country in which they reside and whether they live in an urban or rural area. For this reason, educators attempting to highlight an African identity need to first take the time to find out which specific cultural group(s) their student(s) or their families immigrated from so that overgeneralizing does not occur—which could cause more harm than good.

West Africa. Nana's Cold Days by Adwoa Badoe, illustrated by Bushra Junaid, tells the story of Nana, who leaves warm Africa (likely a country in West Africa given the author's Ghanaian ethnicity) for the colder North America. This children's book does not focus on a specific cultural identity or even country but on the shock of traveling from a warm place to a cold one, making it relatable to children of many different African ethnicities. *Bintou's Braids* by Sylviane Diof, illustrated by Shane W. Evans, tells the story of a West African girl who would like long decorated braids like her older sister. Through the story, she finds out that beauty does not lie within our hairstyles. In both books, the illustrators play with texture, using collage (*Nana's Cold Days*) and vibrant mudcloth and other traditional West African prints (*Bintou's Braids*). A follow-up activity could invite children to play with textures by making a collage with fabrics and paper scraps, stamps, and paint.

East Africa. Babu's Song by Stephanie Stuve-Bodeen, illustrated by Aaron Boyd, is set in Tanzania, an East African country. In this story, the little boy protagonist sells a toy made by his Babu (grandfather) to earn money to buy a soccer ball. *The Matatu* by Eric Walters, illustrated by Eva Campbell, is set in Kenya. Like in *Babu's Song*, the grandfather is also called Babu. For follow-up activities, educators can encourage children to write a story about a day with family or create a market in the dramatic play area to practice counting with money.

Refugees. In addition to centering on different ethnicities, it is also important to normalize the experiences of children with refugee status, especially since they have often witnessed extremely stressful events. The counting book *Counting Kindness: Ten Ways to Welcome Refugee Children*, written by Hollis Kurman and illustrated by Barroux, gives a brief picture of what a child with refugee status might have experienced and how others can help by showing kindness. *Brothers in Hope: The Story of the Lost Boys of Sudan* by Mary Williams, illustrated by R. Gregory Christie, is multi-award-winning true story of human courage and perseverance, focusing on the experiences of some children from Sudan. Teachers can enact social-emotional follow-up activities that teach about empathy, kindness, and pride, among other feelings, for example holding an interactive puppet show during which they tell the story of similar children and have students offer empathetic and kind ways to interact with the puppets. Teachers can also ensure that puppets with refugee status exhibit pride in who they are and where they are from and invite the class to share reasons why they too are proud of their communities.

Being Black and a Member of a Marginalized Religion

According to Pew Research, 79 percent of Black Americans identify as Christian (Masci, Mohamed, and Smith 2018). Many Black people in America experience kinship due to similar religious beliefs, and several Christian denominations are often collectively termed the Black Church. However, 2 percent of Black census respondents indicated that they identify as Muslim. Though this is a small percentage, it makes up the next largest religious affiliation among Black adults in the United States. Additionally, due to migration patterns and social and cultural reasons, certain geographical areas are likely to have more Black Muslims than others. Therefore, although they are a minority, having a Black Muslim in a classroom is a real possibility. Because we often integrate Christian religious practices in schools, with Easter and Christmas celebrations, activities, and school closures, we can also take care to support the developing identities of Black children whose families are a part of marginalized religions. Being that Islam is the only major religion outside of Christianity with a significant number of Black American adherents, resources to support Black Muslim children follow.

Infants and Toddlers

Educators can share books that feature Black Muslims with infants and toddlers. *Baby Touch: Happy Eid!* is a touch-and-feel vocabulary book that features words like *mosque* and *gifts*. One page features *family* as the vocabulary word and shows a Muslim family who has brown skin. Sharing a book such as this can help normalize having multiple marginalized identities. Since *Baby Touch: Happy Eid!* is a touch-and-feel book, the activity is built into the story. After reading each one-word page and showing the pictures, early childhood educators can invite children to touch the pages as they describe together how each item feels. Infant and toddler teachers who do not have access to a book like this could invite a Black Muslim into the classroom to share a culturally affirming read aloud on any topic. Doing either (or both!)

sends the same message of "you are welcome here" and "we appreciate who you are."

Preschoolers

Preschool educators can also read aloud books that feature Muslim characters or families with dark skin. *Mommy's Khimar* by Jamilah Thompkins-Bigelow, illustrated by Ebony Glenn, is about a Black Muslim girl who is in awe of her mother's khimar (a religious hair covering). Being that the hair coverings worn by many Muslim women are often negatively portrayed, this love letter to a mother's khimar serves as a counter to anti-Islamic messages. Another option for celebrating Black Muslim identity and normalizing religious head coverings is *The Proudest Blue: A Story of Hijab and Family* by Ibtihaj Muhammad with S. K. Ali, illustrated by Hatem Aly. The story features a young girl's admiration for her older sister's blue hijab on the first day of school. Following a read aloud with either story, preschoolers can explore different fabrics and create wearable art, such as fabric jewelry, a scarf, a pouch, or something else.

Educators can also read stories about Islamic holidays. *Rashad's Ramadan and Eid al-Fitr* by Lisa Bullard, illustrated by Holli Conger, is a short chapter book that talks about parts of the Islamic faith, like caring about others in need and celebrating Eid. Books like this can be helpful in dispelling myths about what Muslim people actually believe, due to negative portrayals in the media, while also supporting Black Muslim identity because the main family is Black. The book has a built-in follow-up activity: decorating a moon-themed donation can for people in need. It is a common practice for schools to hold canned food drives during traditionally Christian holidays to help families in need, and the same ethos can be applied during Ramadan. A preschool class could create donation cans, collect donations, and contribute to a local charity.

Being Black and Disabled

Having a disability in a world created for able-bodied and typically developing people comes with challenges. Because disabled people are often not considered in any real meaningful way, they face unnecessary challenges throughout their lives. Visibly disabled children also find themselves on the receiving end of curious stares and questions from their peers and adults alike. Children whose disabilities are not visible may face people who express disbelief about whether they have a disability at all or whether they deserve accommodations, and they are even less likely to see their disabilities represented. Coupling a disability with being Black means facing marginalization from ableism and racism at the same time. This state of being a part of multiple marginalized communities can make it difficult to develop positive views about one's identity. Early childhood educators can support their disabled Black children by centering their humanity and experiences in the classrooms through carefully selected read alouds and follow-up activities.

Infants and Toddlers

Meeting Mimi: A Story about Different Abilities by Francie Dolan, illustrated by Wendy Leach, is an easy reader, making it a great short read for tiny attention spans. In the story, a Black girl named Mimi answers questions from peers about her physical disability. The alphabet book *A is for All the Things You Are: A Joyful ABC Book* by Anna Forgerson Hindley, illustrated by Keturah A. Bobo, features positive traits for each letter of the alphabet. The illustrations include racially and ethnically diverse children with various visible disabilities. Infant and toddler teachers can read books such as these and then engage in a discussion about disabilities. Teachers can bring in pictures or miniatures of assistive devices such as wheelchairs, walkers, glasses, hearing aids, and so on, and explain briefly what each is used for.

Preschoolers

Many books for preschoolers talk about disability directly or feature disabled children as the main characters. In keeping with the idea of multiple marginalized identities, three such books that feature Black characters follow. The follow-up activity can be done with any of these three books or any other book that feature a Black child with a disability in a prominent way.

Emmanuel's Dream: The True Story of Emmanuel Ofosu Yeboah by Laurie Ann Thompson, illustrated by Sean Qualls, set in Ghana, West Africa, is about a baby born without the ability to move one of his legs. The story is one of triumph as Emmanuel learns to overcome his physical disability. *My Brother Charlie* by Holly Robinson Peete and Ryan Elizabeth Peete, illustrated by Shane W. Evans, is told from the perspective of a little Black girl whose twin brother is autistic. She describes the ways that they are similar and different. She also describes the great moments and challenges that come with living with her brother Charlie. *Hello Goodbye Dog* by Maria Gianferrari, illustrated by Patrice Barton, tells the story of Zara, a Black girl who uses a wheelchair, and her dog Moose, who does not like goodbyes. In the end, Zara takes Moose to therapy dog school so they can always be together.

Preschool teachers can lead their class in a whole-group discussion that focuses on differences and similarities in the classroom as well as the various strengths and challenges each student faces in their daily lives. This discussion can be written down verbatim, graphed on a large piece of chart paper, or recorded in note form using a pocket chart and index cards. By creating a safe space to talk about differences, educators help protect children with disabilities from harmful behaviors from their peers.

Being Black and a Marginalized Gender

Our society has strict social norms surrounding gender. Many people do not understand or accept the science showing that sex and gender is a spectrum, not a binary of girl and boy, man and woman, or male and female, and because of this, people and children with a gender identity that does not fall neatly on one side of the binary face discrimination. In addition, people who express their gender identity in a way that challenges this binary also face marginalization. For example, boys who prefer to wear dresses or carry purses or girls who do not want to do either of those things can face scrutiny. As with any marginalized identity, when Black children also have a gender identity or expression that does not fit into the socially constructed binary, they face multiplied marginalization. Early childhood educators can help counter the negative messages associated with being a part of a marginalized gender by intentionally creating space for the full spectrum of gender identity and expression to shine in their classrooms.

It is important to note that creating space for expansive genders does not create trans or gender-nonconforming children. Children attend to gender identity in early childhood just as they do race. Discussing and celebrating marginalized genders helps foster understanding about aspects of our world that they are already experiencing. Additionally, it teaches children to care for people regardless of their gender identity, which is critical in our diverse society.

Infants and Toddlers

One way that infant and toddler teachers can create space for multiple genders and gender expressions is to sing gender-inclusive songs. Many times early childhood classrooms overly emphasize gender binaries by separating children into boys and girls, which can teach children early on that there are only two ways to be. By using inclusive language like *children* or *kids* instead of *boys and girls*, educators leave space for all children. By starting children in a gender-inclusive space, we allow them the freedom to be who they are without shame as they get older and learn more about themselves. A few inclusive, easy-to-learn songs follow.

"Good to Be Me" (Sung to the tune of "Here We Go, Loopty Loo")
It is good to be me.
It is good to be you.

Being a kid is cool
Because of the things we can do.

I play with what I want.
I dress in my own clothes.
I give my hair a shake shake shake.
And wear it how it grows.

It is good to be me.
It is good to be you.
Being a kid is cool
Because of the things we can do.

"I Am a Great Kid" (Sung to the tune of "I'm a Little Teapot")
I am a great kid, and so are you.
I can wear pink and I can wear blue.
I am wonderful no matter what I wear.
So let's have fun and play without a care.

"Joy and Smiles" (Sung to the tune of "Head, Shoulders, Knees, and Toes")
Joy, smiles, laughter yeah (laughter yeah),
Joy, smiles, laughter yeah (laughter yeah),
Just being me has me happy as can be.
Joy, smiles, laughter yeah (laughter yeah).

Preschoolers

In addition to using inclusive language and singing inclusive songs, preschool educators can engage their children in read alouds that feature children breaking away from limited views on gender identity and expression. Because preschool children often police gender norms by stating things like "that's for boys" or "only girls can do that," it is quite important for preschool teachers to create an inclusive space that makes room for differences in an explicit way. Engaging in read alouds, discussions, and follow-up activities is a great way to do so.

Allie's Basketball Dream by Barbara Barber, illustrated by Darryl Ligasan, is about a little Black girl, Allie, who receives a basketball as a gift from her father. Allie faces criticism from boys and hears messages from friends that basketball is for boys. Despite this, she continues to play, learning to get better and better. Books like this in which children stand up to limiting gender norms, more specifically books that portray girls engaging in athletic activities, show children that they can follow their passions and interests regardless of their gender. Preschool educators can follow up on the read aloud by letting all children play basketball with preschool-size goals and balls or by using soft balls and hula hoops.

Boys Dance by John Robert Allman, illustrated by Luciano Lozano, features a group of racially diverse boys as they begin ballet lessons. The boys learn about ballet as well as men like them who also studied ballet and other forms of dance and the ways that dancing can benefit boys in other aspects of their lives. Preschool children can experience dance by watching a short online video of a performance from Debbie Allen's Dance Academy or Alvin Ailey's Dance School, both featuring famous and accomplished Black dancers. The children can then imitate the movements they witnessed, dancing to similar music.

Julián Is a Mermaid by Jessica Love celebrates an Afro-Latinx boy with an interest that is often seen as feminine. Julian is celebrated and validated by his grandmother, allowing him to be himself. Preschool educators can allow their children to experience the bliss of being themselves by following up the book with a dress-up parade. Each child can put together a costume made from clothes in the dramatic play center and other bits of fabric or sheets brought in for this exciting experience. After everyone has dressed in their chosen costume, educators play music and allow the children to parade around the classroom.

Reading stories about Black children engaging in activities that push the boundaries of what it means to be a boy or a girl supports children with a range of ways to express their gender. These sorts of books give children permission to pursue their interests regardless of what others think is appropriate for their gender. This endorsement supports the healthy development of Black children with marginalized genders or gender expressions because it lets them see that they do not have to change who they are.

On the other hand, Black trans children can benefit from representation that shows that it *is* OK to change so you can be who you are. A book like *It Feels Good to Be Yourself: A Book about Gender Identity* by Theresa Thorn, illustrated by Noah Grigni, does a great job of transmitting that message. The book features a racially diverse cast of characters, including a biracial child and a Black child who uses a wheelchair. Thorn uses simple, child-friendly language to discuss gender identity words and concepts, including *transgender*, *cisgender* (not trans), and having multiple nonbinary identities. Preschool educators could follow up this read aloud, or a similar one, with a gender showcase. Each child can use art supplies, cut-up magazines, and construction paper to create a gender collage. Educators can encourage children to include anything that tells who they are or what they like, be it boy, girl, both, or neither. Children can then share their work with a small group of peers.

Being Black and a Part of a Minority Family Type

The idea that the nuclear family is the standard family type is quite pervasive, even today. Two-parent households, with parents of opposite genders who live alone with their biological children, continue to be the most common representation of "family" in the United States. However, we know that, in reality, families are composed of many different combinations of people (and pets!). Children who are a part of families that fall outside of the nuclear family type can benefit from extra support. Some marginalized family types include same-gender parents, adoptive parents, single parents, children being raised by grandparents, and multigenerational homes. Young Black children can be a part of any of these family types and therefore can benefit from supportive educators who take the time to represent them in the classroom.

Infants and Toddlers

Families Can by Dan Saks, illustrated by Brooke Smart, shows different types of families engaging in activities like going to the park and playing games. It features same-gender parents, multiracial parents, immigrant parents, and grandparents as caregivers. Teachers can read this or a similar book, like *The Family Book* by Todd Parr, at the beginning of their time with children, asking each family for a family picture. Teachers can talk about the different families in the classroom before, during, or after reading the book.

Highlighting same-gender parents, *Baby's First Words* by Stella Blackstone and Sunny Scribens, illustrated by Christiane Engel, is a vocabulary book designed for infants and toddlers. The items in the environment of the book, such as *towel*, *car*, and *dog*, are labeled to help young children learn the words to common objects. We learn about the items in the environment as a baby goes throughout her day, waking up, exploring, eating, and going to bed with her two fathers, one of whom is a Black man. Infant and toddler teachers can extend this book by bringing in some real objects that are highlighted in the text, to help with vocabulary acquisition through concrete items.

Use *Go Grandma Go!* by Lynn Plourde, illustrated by Sophie Beer, to highlight multigenerational homes or grandparents raising their grandchildren. The board book shows diverse grandmas and their grandchildren enjoying their time together. One Black grandma takes her grandchild shopping for food and other items. In a follow-up activity, give the children little bags to fill up to pretend they are going shopping. Teachers can also consider inviting grandparents into the classroom to read to the children.

Preschoolers

Best Best Colors/Los Mejores Colores by Eric Hoffman, illustrated by Celeste Henriquez, is a bilingual (English and Spanish) book that features a Black child with two mothers. *And That's Why She's My Mama* by Tiarra Nazario, illustrated by Gabby Correia, is a book about diverse adoptive families. The book is told from the perspective of many children explaining why their adoptive mother is their mama. In *A Father Like That* by Charlotte Zolotow, illustrated by LeUyen Pham, the narrator is a Black boy telling his single mother what it would be like if his father was there. The book ends with his mother telling him that he can be a father like that when he grows up. *Sunday Shopping* by Sally Derby, illustrated by Shadra Strickland, follows a little Black girl as she goes shopping with her grandmother. This beautiful story with AAL dialogue supports Black preschoolers in multigenerational homes and those being raised by grandparents.

Each of the four books mentioned supports a different type of marginalized family in a way that also supports Black children. Preschool educators can read these or other books with their students to normalize the diversity of family structures found in our society. As with infants and toddlers, tying the books back to the children's actual families is a great follow-up activity. Teachers can ask families to bring in pictures, and then each child can use that picture as the cover for their own family book, in which they use their developing literacy and art skills to write and illustrate a story about their family. The finished books can be placed in a basket in the library area so children can see the diversity of the families within their classroom.

Being Black and Low Income

Despite the many early childhood programs and services designed to serve low-income families, curriculum materials only infrequently represent these families. Middle-class families are overwhelmingly represented in children's curricular materials, especially children's books. Early childhood educators can work to meet the needs of their students while also embracing the communities and homes from which the children come, seeking out books that overtly discuss economic issues as well as books that feature settings that are familiar for some low-income children and their families. Sharing these books with the class can help children who are marginalized due to both race and economic class feel more confident in themselves.

Infants and Toddlers

You Matter by Christian Robinson is a beautifully illustrated book with diverse characters and very little text, making it perfect for an infant or toddler class. It does not explicitly discuss anyone's economic status, although the setting is urban and we see the outside of an apartment building as well as public transportation on the road. Being that most children's books take place in houses and what seem to be suburban areas, this difference in setting makes connections for children living in apartment complexes and children who take public transportation.

In addition to reading books, infant and toddler teachers can also make a point of teaching vocabulary words for many types of homes. Infant and toddler educators can also bring in pictures and models of mobile homes, apartments, duplexes, shelters, and other relevant homes to help to normalize diverse living arrangements at a young age. The same can be done for transportation words. Going beyond common vocabulary words such as cars, trucks, airplanes, and trains, infant and toddler teachers can center the experiences of some children from low-income families by also including city buses, interstate buses, bicycles, and walking as valid forms of transportation.

Preschoolers

There are many books appropriate for preschoolers that feature Black characters engaging in life with limited financial means. Preschool teachers can select any of these sorts of books to engage in a read aloud and have a discussion with the class about connections to their lives. For example, *The Fair Housing Five and the Haunted House*, written by the Greater New Orleans Fair Housing Action Center and illustrated by Sharika Mahdi, tells the story of a family looking for housing. Students who have experienced apartment hunting with their families may be able to talk about what that was like for them.

Creating space for children to share their experiences and make meaningful connections to the lives of characters like them is empowering. Reading and discussing a book like *The Fair Housing Five and the Haunted House* can help make multiple marginalized children feel seen. The experience also lets children practice expressive and receptive oral language skills. For a further extension, preschool teachers can follow the discussion and read aloud with an art activity in which children paint the way they feel. In this way, if the discussion makes anyone upset, the children have a positive outlet for their emotions.

Additional stories to consider

Happy Like Soccer by Maribeth Boelts, illustrated by Lauren Castillo

Last Stop on Market Street by Matt De La Peña, illustrated by Christian Robinson

A Shelter in Our Car by Monica Gunning, illustrated by Elaine Pedlar

Discussion Questions

1. How might you learn about the multiple identities of your children and their families?
2. What gifts and talents do your multiple marginalized families have that they can bring into the classroom? How might you find out?
3. What other identities could you account for in your plans to fully support the developing identities of the children in your care?
4. How could you partner with families to send positive messages to children about their identities?

5. How could you partner with the larger community to send positive messages to children about their identities?
6. What could you say to families who have questions about supporting the range of identities in your classroom?
7. What resources do you have to help you learn more about different marginalized identities?
8. What steps could you take to stop identity-based marginalization when you see it happening around you?

The Power of Racially Affirming Practice

A PERSONAL STORY

When my husband and I had our first child, he had recently been honorably discharged from the US Air Force and was attending the local state university. His college student status granted us access to the university's child development center. The center was accredited by the National Association for the Education of Young Children (NAEYC) and had been for years. Apart from the wonderful characteristics of a NAEYC-accredited center (well-educated teachers, developmentally appropriate curriculum, low staff turnover, a parent advisory group, and more), the center had a great deal of racial and ethnic diversity, as compared to centers across the city. These demographics were largely because enrollment was limited to faculty, staff, and students of this public university with nearly thirty thousand undergraduate students. Not only were the children enrolled diverse, but so too were the teachers. Further, diversity did not just exist at the center. It was celebrated and intentionally included in the curriculum.

This focus on human diversity was important to us because we made great efforts at home to help ensure that our child would feel valued and like she belonged in society. We were both cognizant of anti-Black societal messages and therefore made it our mission to create a home environment that was unapologetically celebratory of Blackness. At the time, we thought the home environment that we created would be enough to foster a love for self, but our knowing that the child development center celebrated human diversity was a plus.

While she attended the child development center, my daughter thrived. She was confident, happy, and well-adjusted. It was her home away from home. She began at the center when she was six weeks old, and once she made it to a preschool classroom, we could tell she had grown confident in herself.

One day she came home from school and asked me if I would put beads in her hair. Even though braids and twists with beads on the end is a typical hairstyle for Black children of her age, it was not one that I had ever installed on her hair. I figured she had seen another Black girl or two wearing her hair in this way and wanted her hair done to match. I thought it was cute that she wanted to wear her hair this way, as I remembered when I was young being enamored of my friend's beads and feeling happy when I wore them myself. I went to the store and purchased beads for her and began adorning her braids and twists with colorful plastic and natural wooden beads, instead of the barrettes and elastics from before. Adding beads to her braids and twists made styling her hair take longer, but I was willing to do it because of the way she responded each time I finished that week's style. She loved her hair. She would dance to make her beads click together. She would video chat with her grandparents and ask them if they liked her hair while flipping her twists or shaking her head. I have videos on my phone of her joyfully swinging her head back and forth. I loved seeing her love herself.

One day I mentioned her hair love to the lead teacher in the room. The veteran White teacher explained to me that they had read the story *I Love My Hair!* by Natasha Tarpley and then pretended to style each other's hair in the dramatic play center. She said my daughter really enjoyed the activity, so it made sense that she would respond in such a positive way to wearing one of the hairstyles that the Black girl protagonist described in the book. I had known that my daughter wanted to wear beads because of something that happened in the center, but I had no idea that it stemmed from her teacher, a White teacher at that, planning a lesson for her group of diverse students that highlighted hair just like my daughter's. I am eternally grateful to her for seeing the importance of focusing on an aspect of Black racial identity that is so often negatively portrayed and turning it into a positive learning experience.

The teacher had read an article, and instead of just going on as usual, she chose to implement into her classrooms what she had read. She was a phenomenal teacher, but this was not unique to her. The educators at the child development center were committed to positive learning experiences and creating classroom environments that fostered the healthy development of all children. Just as my Black child was thriving, so were the other children. Taking time to focus on lessons for specific groups did not harm any students who were not the focus at the moment. Instead, the children were able to embrace who they were and who others were as well.

For equity reasons, the university child development center had a limit on how long a family could remain enrolled. So although my husband was now in graduate school and still a student, we had to find a new place for our children to learn and grow. We said goodbye to the teachers and staff whom we had connected with over the years and enrolled our two children into a private early childhood school.

After many interviews and school tours I selected this particular school because it was on acres of wooded and grassy land. Deer frequently walked by as the children safely learned and played in the school buildings. I felt my children would thrive in this school that emphasized outdoor play, a connection to nature, and a challenging curriculum. I noticed there were not many BI&POC children enrolled, but I thought that with our home environment that was intentionally designed to foster a love for our people and culture and with the foundation set by the university child development center, it would be enough to keep our children developing in a healthy way. When I noticed there were no Black dolls in the classrooms, I brought in about a dozen Black dolls that the center staff graciously accepted. They explained they had not noticed the lack of representation and agreed that it was important. But the problem was bigger than dolls. They had not noticed the lack of Black dolls because the school curriculum and teaching dispositions did not account for human diversity. It was not acknowledged, celebrated, nor built into lessons. The school defaulted on representing the White middle-class perspective and essentially ignoring all others, whether intentionally or not.

My girls were enrolled in the nature-centered private school for a few months when my eldest daughter started to communicate changes in her developing racial identity. One evening when I sat in my bed snuggled up with my children, the following exchange occurred.

"Mama, I don't want my dark skin."

"What? I love your dark skin."

"Well, you can have it."

My heart sank. My daughter who would call her grandparents just to show off her new cultural hairstyle was now saying that I could have her skin. On a later date, when I was dropping my children off at school, she looked out of the car window, seeing her school building, and said to me that she wished she had blue eyes. I told her I loved her beautiful brown eyes and she responded with silence as she continued looking at the school grounds.

She did not just verbalize wanting to be different. These desires also manifested in her play. She would pretend to have long flowing hair, as many White people do, by draping a towel on her head. When I asked her about her hairstyle and pointed out that our hair did not hang down like that, she responded that she was pretending to be White. My little girl could not only identify what she did not like about her that made her a Black person, but she could also articulate the exact type of person she wished that she was.

This abrupt change in my daughter's feelings about herself broke my heart, but it also taught me a lesson, a lesson that I have made my mission to share with others. Educators have a powerful opportunity to influence the way that children feel about themselves. The Black art, books, television shows, toys, festivals, and other experiences that my husband and I provided for our children were not enough. Our home environment did not change in its celebration of our culture—only her school environment had changed. But that change profoundly affected her, and she is not an anomaly. Of course, her teachers at school had no idea that she was struggling with her identity. They saw a child who was eager to play, performed well on assessments, and had no trouble following the rules. They saw a child who wanted to hug her teacher and waved goodbye with a smile on her face. However, when she was home, where she felt the safest, the smile would disappear as she spoke of her desire to be different.

This difference between how she presented herself at school and how she behaved at home is important to consider. When I speak of the harm of "color-blind" practices, it can be easy to dismiss it as hyperbole because educators often are not privy to the real feelings that children have about themselves. A smiling child is not necessarily a confident child, and a seemingly confident child is not necessarily a child who loves and embraces their social identities. Further, if our home was not a place in which we openly spoke about race and racial differences, my daughter may not have felt comfortable revealing her racial thoughts to me either. As adults, we have the power to create environments in which children feel like they can be their whole and authentic selves—or not.

My daughter is fine now. We eventually disenrolled our children from the school and homeschooled them until we found a school that celebrated Blackness as part of the curriculum. We worked to undo the harm caused by "color-blind" curricula and teaching practices, but we never should have had to do so.

Of course, *my* daughter was fine. She has a mother who is an early childhood educator, taught in a model school, trained early childhood educators in this topic and others, and eventually sought a PhD focusing on this very topic. She is not the typical young child. She was positioned to overcome schooling that never considered her. I had the privilege to be able to change schools, to sell my house and move to a more diverse area, to provide diverse materials for the school, to find a private independent Black school, to give her future teachers books, and to train the entire faculty at her elementary school.

But my child being fine is not enough.

I want *every* child to walk into *any* school and leave with confidence and knowledge of how wonderful they and their racial/ethnic group members are. Black children should be able to enjoy what White children feel as they are routinely centered. My hope is that no young child comes home wanting to give away their dark skin, that no three-year-old will sit in their car seat, looking onto school grounds, wishing their beautiful brown eyes were blue. I want all young children to be able to thrive and feel comfortable in their skin. I want children to be able to look in the mirror and confidently say "I like myself" because they were given the proper support to do so, even while they are developing in a society that so often tells them to believe differently. I want early childhood educators to tap into their power and harness it to foster positive racial identity development in their Black students. The children need you to have the audacity to not only care but also to take action.

My hope is that this book will get you started on your journey in fostering positive racial identity if your journey has not yet begun. If you are already on a path to fostering positive racial identity, my goal is that this book will move you forward. My desire is that your teaching practices will continue to grow and that each child who enters your classroom leaves your care having developed in a healthy and positive way. I am confident that early childhood educators can use their power to counter the common anti-Blackness that exists in our society until the day that it no longer exists. Will you join me in creating a future where developing healthily as a Black child is not such a feat? The children need you.

Discussion Questions

1. In thinking of the students in your classroom, do you know how any of them feel about their own identities? Why or why not?
2. How could you have conversations with parents about this topic?
3. What does your physical environment currently communicate about who is important and valuable?

4. What could you do to form relationships with students to help them feel comfortable sharing their feelings about racial identity?
5. Who in your network could help you along this journey of fostering positive racial identity?

RECOMMENDED CHILDREN'S BOOKS

Adoff, Arnold. 2002. *Black Is Brown Is Tan*. Illustrated by Emily Arnold McCully. New York: HarperCollins.

Ahn, Courtney. 2021. *A Little Book about Activism*. Portland, OR: A Kids Book About.

Allman, John Robert. 2020. *Boys Dance*. Illustrated by Luciano Lozano. New York: Doubleday.

Arnold, Marsha Diane. 2016. *A Welcome Song for Baby*. Illustrated by Sophie Allsopp. London: Tamarind.

Ashman, Linda. 2016. *Henry Wants More*. Illustrated by Brooke Boynton Hughes. New York: Random House.

Asim, Jabari. 2010. *Girl of Mine*. Illustrated by LeUyen Pham. New York: LB Kids.

Asim, Jabari. 2019. *Whose Knees Are These?* Illustrated by LeUyen Pham. New York: LB Kids.

Asim, Jabari. 2019. *Whose Toes Are Those?* Illustrated by LeUyen Pham. New York: LB Kids.

Atinuke. 2019. *Baby Goes to Market*. Illustrated by Angela Brooksbank. Somerville, MA: Candlewick.

Atinuke. 2021. *Baby, Sleepy Baby.* Illustrated by Angela Brooksbank. Somerville, MA: Candlewick.

Badoe, Adwoa. 2002. *Nana's Cold Days.* Illustrated by Bushra Junaid. Toronto, ON: Groundwood Books.

Baptist, Kelly J. 2021. *The Electric Slide and Kai.* Illustrated by Darnell Johnson. New York: Lee & Low Books.

Barber, Barbara. 2013. *Allie's Basketball Dream.* Paperback edition. Illustrated by Darryl Ligasan. New York: Lee & Low Books.

Barnes, Derrick. 2017. *Crown: An Ode to the Fresh Cut.* Illustrated by Gordon C. James. Chicago: Bolden, an Agate imprint.

Beaty, Andrea. 2016. *Ada Twist, Scientist.* Illustrated by David Roberts. New York: Abrams Books for Young Readers.

Beauvais, Garcelle, and Sebastian A. Jones. 2013. *I Am Mixed.* Illustrated by James C. Webster. Los Angeles: Stranger Comics.

Benjamin, Floella. 2009. *My Two Grannies.* Illustrated by Margaret Chamberlain. London: Frances Lincoln Children's Books.

Blackstone, Stella, and Sunny Scribens. 2019. *Baby's First Words.* Illustrated by Christiane Engel. Cambridge, MA: Barefoot Books.

Boelts, Maribeth. 2012. *Happy Like Soccer.* Illustrated by Lauren Castillo. Somerville, MA: Candlewick.

Brantley-Newton, Vanessa. 2019. *Grandma's Purse.* Illustrated by Vanessa Brantley-Newton. New York: Alfred A. Knopf.

Brown, Lisa. 2016. *The Airport Book.* New York: Roaring Brook Press.

Brown, Tameka Fryer. 2020. *Brown Baby Lullaby.* Illustrated by A. G. Ford. New York: Farrar, Straus and Giroux.

Browne, Mahogany L. 2018. *Woke Baby.* Illustrated by Theodore Taylor III. New York: Roaring Brook Press.

Bullard, Lisa. 2012. *Rashad's Ramadan and Eid al-Fitr.* Illustrated by Holli Conger. Minneapolis: Millbrook Press.

Bynum, Betty K. 2013. *I'm a Pretty Little Black Girl!* Illustrated by Claire Armstrong Parod. Los Angeles: Dreamtitle.

Chacko, Ashwin. 2021. *A Little Book about Justice*. Portland, OR: A Kids Book About.

Cherry, Matthew A. 2019. *Hair Love*. Illustrated by Vashti Harrison. New York: Kokila.

Cooke, Trish. 2003. *Full, Full, Full of Love*. Illustrated by Paul Howard. Cambridge, MA: Candlewick.

Cummings, Pat. 1998. *My Aunt Came Back*. Illustrated by Pat Cummings. New York: HarperCollins.

Damluji, Mona. 2021. *Together*. Illustrated by Innosanta Nagara. New York: Seven Stories Press.

Danticat, Edwidge. 2019. *My Mommy Medicine*. Illustrated by Shannon Wright. New York: Roaring Brook Press.

De La Peña, Matt. 2015. *Last Stop on Market Street*. Illustrated by Christian Robinson. New York: G. P. Putnam's Sons.

Derby, Sally. 2015. *Sunday Shopping*. Illustrated by Shadra Strickland. New York: Lee & Low Books.

Díaz, Junot. 2018. *Islandborn*. Illustrated by Leo Espinosa. New York: Dial Books.

Diggs, Taye. 2015. *Mixed Me!* Illustrated by Shane W. Evans. New York: Feiwel and Friends.

Diof, Sylviane A. 2001. *Bintou's Braids*. Illustrated by Shane W. Evans. San Francisco: Chronicle Books.

Dolan, Francie. 2020. *Meeting Mimi: A Story about Different Abilities*. Illustrated by Wendy Leach. Vero Beach, FL: Rourke Educational Media.

Duncan, Alice Faye. 2005. *Honey Baby Sugar Child*. Illustrated by Susan Keeter. New York: Simon & Schuster Books for Young Readers.

Ewing, Chana Ginelle. 2020. *An ABC of Equality*. Illustrated by Paulina Morgan. London: Frances Lincoln Children's Books.

Falwell, Cathryn. 2008. *Feast for 10*. Illustrated by Cathryn Falwell. New York: Clarion.

Fields, Monique. 2019. *Honeysmoke: A Story of Finding Your Color.* Illustrated by Yesenia Moises. New York: Imprint.

Frame, Jeron Ashford. 2003. *Yesterday I Had the Blues.* Illustrated by R. Gregory Christie. Berkley, CA: Tricycle Press.

Frederick, Malcolm. 2008. *Kamal Goes to Trinidad.* Illustrated by Prodeepta Das. London: Frances Lincoln Children's Books.

Garton, Liz. 2015. *All the World.* Board book edition. Illustrated by Marla Frazee. New York: Little Simon.

Gianferrari, Maria. 2017. *Hello Goodbye Dog.* Illustrated by Patrice Barton. New York: Roaring Brook Press.

Gordon, Charnaie. 2020. *A Kids Book about Diversity.* Portland, OR: A Kids Book About.

Gorman, Amanda. 2021. *Change Sings: A Children's Anthem.* Illustrated by Loren Long. New York: Viking.

Graham, Bob. 2005. *Oscar's Half Birthday.* Illustrated by Bob Graham. Cambridge, MA: Candlewick.

Greater New Orleans Fair Housing Action Center. 2010. *The Fair Housing Five and the Haunted House.* Illustrated by Sharika Mahdi. CreateSpace Independent Publishing Platform.

Greenfield, Eloise. 1993. *She Come Bringing Me That Little Baby Girl.* Reprint edition. Illustrated by John Steptoe. New York: HarperCollins.

Gunning, Monica. 2013. *A Shelter in Our Car.* Paperback edition. Illustrated by Elaine Pedlar. New York: Lee & Low Books.

Hamanaka, Sheila. 1994. *All the Colors of the Earth.* Illustrated by Sheila Hamanaka. New York: Morrow Junior.

Harris, Robie H. 2018. *Who? A Celebration of Babies.* Illustrated by Natascha Rosenberg. New York: Abrams Appleseed.

Harrison, Vashti. 2017. *Little Leaders: Bold Women in Black History.* Illustrated by Vashti Harrison. New York: Little, Brown and Company.

Harrison, Vashti. 2018. *Dream Big, Little One.* Illustrated by Vashti Harrison. New York: Little, Brown and Company.

Harrison, Vashti. 2018. *Little Dreamers: Visionary Women around the World.* Illustrated by Vashti Harrison. New York: Little, Brown and Company.

Harrison, Vashti. 2019. *Little Legends: Exceptional Men in Black History.* Illustrated by Vashti Harrison. New York: Little, Brown and Company.

Harrison, Vashti. 2019. *Think Big, Little One.* Illustrated by Vashti Harrison. New York: Little, Brown and Company.

Harrison, Vashti. 2020. *Follow Your Dreams, Little One.* Illustrated by Vashti Harrison. New York: Little, Brown and Company.

Hindley, Anna Forgerson. 2019. *A Is for All the Things You Are: A Joyful ABC Book.* Illustrated by Keturah A. Bobo. Washington, DC: Smithsonian Books.

Hoffman, Eric. 1999. *Best Best Colors/Los Mejores Colores.* Illustrated by Celeste Henriquez. St. Paul, MN: Redleaf Press.

Hohn, Nadia L. 2016. *Malaika's Costume.* Illustrated by Irene Luxbacher. Toronto, ON: Groundwood Books.

hooks, bell. 1999. *Happy to Be Nappy.* Illustrated by Chris Raschka. New York: Hyperion.

hooks, bell. 2002. *Be Boy Buzz.* Illustrated by Chris Raschka. New York: Hyperion.

Hughes, Langston. 2013. *Lullaby (for a Black Mother).* Illustrated by Sean Qualls. New York: Harcourt Children's Books.

Hughes, Langston. 2021. *Lullaby for a Black Mother.* Board book edition. Illustrated by Sean Qualls. New York: Clarion.

Isadora, Rachel. 2008. *Peekaboo Morning.* Board book edition. Illustrated by Rachel Isadora. New York: G. P. Putnam's Sons.

Johnson, Angela. 1994. *Joshua by the Sea.* Illustrated by Rhonda Mitchell. New York: Orchard Books.

Johnson, Angela. 1997. *Daddy Calls Me Man.* Illustrated by Rhonda Mitchell. New York: Orchard Books.

Johnson, Angela. 2004. *Just Like Josh Gibson.* Illustrated by Beth Peck. New York: Simon & Schuster Books for Young Readers.

Joy, Angela. 2020. *Black Is a Rainbow Color.* Illustrated by Ekua Holmes. New York: Roaring Brook Press.

Juster, Norton. 2005. *The Hello Goodbye Window.* Illustrated by Chris Raschka. New York: Michael di Capua Books/Hyperion.

Katz, Karen. 1999. *The Colors of Us.* Illustrated by Karen Katz. New York: Henry Holt and Company.

Katz, Karen. 2008. *Ten Tiny Tickles.* Board book edition. Illustrated by Karen Katz. New York: Little Simon.

Keats, Ezra Jack. 1978. *The Trip.* Illustrated by Ezra Jack Keats. New York: Greenwillow.

Keats, Ezra Jack. 1998. *Goggles!* Illustrated by Ezra Jack Keats. New York: Puffin Books.

Keats, Ezra Jack. 1998. *A Letter to Amy.* Illustrated by Ezra Jack Keats. New York: Viking Books for Young Readers.

Keats, Ezra Jack. 1998. *Peter's Chair.* Illustrated by Ezra Jack Keats. New York: Viking Books for Young Readers.

Keats, Ezra Jack. 1998. *Whistle for Willie.* Illustrated by Ezra Jack Keats. New York: Viking Books for Young Readers.

Keats, Ezra Jack. 1999. *Hi, Cat!* Illustrated by Ezra Jack Keats. New York: Viking Books for Young Readers.

Keats, Ezra Jack. 2001. *Pet Show!* Illustrated by Ezra Jack Keats. New York: Puffin Books.

Keats, Ezra Jack. 2002. *Keats's Neighborhood.* Illustrated by Ezra Jack Keats. New York: Viking Books for Young Readers.

Keats, Ezra Jack. 2011. *The Snowy Day.* 50th anniversary edition. Illustrated by Ezra Jack Keats. New York: Viking.

Kendi, Ibram X. 2020. *Antiracist Baby.* Illustrated by Ashley Lukashevsky. New York: Kokila.

Kissinger, Katie. 2014. *All the Colors We Are: The Story of How We Get Our Skin Color.* St. Paul, MN: Redleaf Press.

Kurman, Hollis. 2020. *Counting Kindness: Ten Ways to Welcome Refugee Children*. Illustrated by Barroux. Watertown, MA: Charlesbridge.

Ladybird. 2021. *Baby Touch: Happy Eid!* New York: Ladybird.

Lee, Spike, and Tonya Lewis Lee. 2005. *Please, Puppy, Please*. Illustrated by Kadir Nelson. New York: Simon & Schuster Books for Young Readers.

Lee, Spike, and Tonya Lewis Lee. 2007. *Please, Baby, Please*. Board book edition. Illustrated by Kadir Nelson. New York: Little Simon.

Light, Steve. 2018. *Black Bird Yellow Sun*. Illustrated by Steve Light. Somerville, MA: Candlewick.

Love, Jessica. 2018. *Julián Is a Mermaid*. Illustrated by Jessica Love. Somerville, MA: Candlewick.

Manning, Maurie J. 2008. *Kitchen Dance*. Illustrated by Maurie J. Manning. Somerville, MA: Clarion Books.

Marley, Cedella. 2014. *One Love*. Board book edition. Illustrated by Vanessa Brantley-Newton. San Francisco: Chronicle Books.

Marley, Cedella. 2015. *Every Little Thing*. Board book edition. Illustrated by Vanessa Brantley-Newton. San Francisco: Chronicle Books.

McAllister, Margaret. 2015. *15 Things Not to Do with a Baby*. Illustrated by Holly Sterling. London: Frances Lincoln Children's Books.

McKissack, Patricia. 1986. *Flossie and the Fox*. Illustrated by Rachel Isadora. New York: Dial Books.

McQuinn, Anna. 2006. *Lola at the Library*. Illustrated by Rosalind Beardshaw. Watertown, MA: Charlesbridge.

McQuinn, Anna. 2010. *Lola Loves Stories*. Illustrated by Rosalind Beardshaw. Watertown, MA: Charlesbridge.

McQuinn, Anna. 2012. *Lola Reads to Leo*. Illustrated by Rosalind Beardshaw. Watertown, MA: Charlesbridge.

McQuinn, Anna. 2014. *Leo Loves Baby Time*. Illustrated by Ruth Hearson. Watertown, MA: Charlesbridge.

McQuinn, Anna. 2014. *Lola Plants a Garden*. Illustrated by Rosalind Beardshaw. Watertown, MA: Charlesbridge.

McQuinn, Anna. 2016. *Leo Can Swim*. Illustrated by Ruth Hearson. Watertown, MA: Charlesbridge.

McQuinn, Anna. 2017. *Lola Gets a Cat*. Illustrated by Rosalind Beardshaw. Watertown, MA: Charlesbridge.

McQuinn, Anna. 2018. *Leo Gets a Checkup*. Illustrated by Ruth Hearson. Watertown, MA: Charlesbridge.

McQuinn, Anna. 2019. *Lola Goes to School*. Illustrated by Rosalind Beardshaw. Watertown, MA: Charlesbridge.

McQuinn, Anna. 2021. *Leo Loves Daddy*. Illustrated by Ruth Hearson. Watertown, MA: Charlesbridge.

McQuinn, Anna. 2021. *Leo Loves Mommy*. Illustrated by Ruth Hearson. Watertown, MA: Charlesbridge.

McQuinn, Anna. 2021. *Lola Sleeps Over*. Illustrated by Rosalind Beardshaw. Watertown, MA: Charlesbridge.

Memory, Jelani. 2019. *A Kids Book about Racism*. Portland, OR: A Kids Book About.

Memory, Jelani. 2021. *A Little Book about Racism*. Portland, OR: A Kids Book About.

Millar, Goldie, and Lisa A. Berger. 2014. *F Is for Feelings*. Illustrated by Hazel Mitchell. Minneapolis: Free Spirit Publishing.

Miller, Sharee. 2017. *Princess Hair*. Illustrated by Sharee Miller. New York: Little, Brown and Company.

Miller, Sharee. 2018. *Don't Touch My Hair!* Illustrated by Sharee Miller. New York: Little, Brown and Company.

Morrison, Toni, with Slade Morrison. 2009. *Peeny Butter Fudge*. Illustrated by Joe Cepeda. New York: Simon & Schuster.

Muhammad, Ibtihaj, and S. K. Ali. 2019. *The Proudest Blue: A Story of Hijab and Family*. Illustrated by Hatem Aly. New York: Little, Brown and Company.

Nagara, Innosanto. 2013. *A Is for Activist*. Illustrated by Innosanto Nagara. New York: Seven Stories Press.

Nagara, Innosanto. 2015. *Counting on Community*. Illustrated by Innosanto Nagara. New York: Seven Stories Press.

Nazario, Tiarra. 2018. *And That's Why She's My Mama*. Illustrated by Gabby Correia. N.p.: And That's Why Children's Books.

Nyong'o, Lupita. 2018. *Sulwe*. Illustrated by Vashti Harrison. New York: Simon & Schuster Books for Young Readers.

Parr, Todd. 2019. *The Family Book*. Board book edition. Illustrated by Todd Parr. New York: LB Kids.

Peete, Holly Robinson, and Ryan Elizabeth Peete. 2010. *My Brother Charlie*. Illustrated by Shane W. Evans. New York: Scholastic.

Pinkney, Andrea. 2021. *Count to Love*. Illustrated by Brian Pinkney. New York: Cartwheel Books.

Pinkney, Sandra L. 2006. *Shades of Black: A Celebration of Our Children*. Board book edition. New York: Cartwheel Books.

Plourde, Lynn. 2020. *Go Grandma Go!* Illustrated by Sophie Beer. New York: Little Simon.

Raschka, Chris. 2007. *Yo! Yes?* Illustrated by Chris Raschka. New York: Scholastic.

Recio, Sili. 2020. *If Dominican Were a Color*. Illustrated by Brianna McCarthy. New York: Simon & Schuster Books for Young Readers.

Redd, Nancy. 2020. *Bedtime Bonnet*. Illustrated by Nneka Myers. New York: Random House Books for Young Readers.

Redding, LaTisha. 2016. *Calling the Water Drum*. Illustrated by Aaron Boyd. New York: Lee & Low Books.

Ringgold, Faith. 1999. *Counting to Tar Beach*. Illustrated by Faith Ringgold. New York: Crown Publishers.

Robinson, Christian. 2020. *You Matter*. Illustrated by Christian Robinson. New York: Atheneum Books for Young Readers.

Roe, Mechal Renee. 2019. *Happy Hair*. Illustrated by Mechal Renee Roe. New York: Doubleday.

Roe, Mechal Renee. 2020. *Cool Cuts*. Illustrated by Mechal Renee Roe. New York: Doubleday.

Rose, Tiffany. 2019. *M Is for Melanin: A Celebration of the Black Child*. Illustrated by Tiffany Rose. New York: Little Bee Books.

Saks, Dan. 2021. *Families Can*. Illustrated by Brooke Smart. New York: Rise x Penguin Workshop.

Schofield-Morrison, Connie. 2014. *I Got the Rhythm*. Illustrated by Frank Morrison. New York: Bloomsbury.

Stewart, Whitney. 2020. *Rest & Relax/Descansa Y Relájate*. Illustrated by Rocío Alejandro. Cambridge, MA: Barefoot Books.

Stuve-Bodeen, Stephanie. 2003. *Babu's Song*. Illustrated by Aaron Boyd. New York: Lee & Low Books.

Tarpley, Natasha Anastasia. 1998. *I Love My Hair!* Illustrated by E. B. Lewis. New York: Little, Brown and Company.

Thierry, Jordan. 2020. *A Kids Book about Systemic Racism*. Portland, OR: A Kids Book About.

Thompkins-Bigelow, Jamilah. 2018. *Mommy's Khimar*. Illustrated by Ebony Glenn. New York: Salaam Reads/Simon & Schuster Books for Young Readers.

Thompson, Laurie Ann. 2015. *Emmanuel's Dream: The True Story of Emmanuel Ofosu Yeboah*. Illustrated by Sean Qualls. New York: Schwartz & Wade.

Thorn, Theresa. 2019. *It Feels Good to Be Yourself: A Book about Gender Identity*. Illustrated by Noah Grigni. New York: Henry Holt and Company.

Tyler, Michael. 2005. *The Skin You Live In*. Illustrated by David Lee Csicsko. Chicago: Chicago Children's Museum.

Van Camp, Richard. 2013. *Little You*. Illustrated by Julie Flett. Victoria, BC: Orca Book Publishers.

Venus, Pamela. 2008. *Let's Feed the Ducks*. Illustrated by Pamela Venus. London: Firetree Books.

Walters, Eric. 2016. *The Matatu*. Illustrated by Eva Campbell. Custer, WA: Orca Book Publishers.

Williams, Mary. 2005. *Brothers in Hope: The Story of the Lost Boys of Sudan.* Illustrated by R. Gregory Christie. New York: Lee & Low Books.

Williams, Vera B. 1997. *"More More More," Said the Baby.* Board book edition. Illustrated by Vera B. Williams. New York: HarperFestival.

Wilson-Max, Ken. 2020. *Where's Lenny?* Illustrated by Ken Wilson-Max. Tulsa: Kane Miller, a Division of EDC Publishing.

Winstanley, Nicola. 2011. *Cinnamon Baby.* Illustrated by Janice Nadeau. Boston: Kids Can Press.

Zolotow, Charlotte. 2007. *A Father Like That.* Illustrated by LeUyen Pham. New York: HarperCollins.

REFERENCES

Alanís, Iliana, Iheoma U. Iruka, eds., and Susan Friedman. 2021. *Advancing Equity and Embracing Diversity in Early Childhood Education: Elevating Voices and Actions.* Washington, DC: National Association for the Education of Young Children.

Alim, H. Samy, and Geneva Smitherman. 2012. *Articulate While Black: Barack Obama, Language, and Race in the U.S.* New York: Oxford University Press.

Bell, Yvonne R., and Tangela R. Clark. 1998. "Culturally Relevant Reading Material as Related to Comprehension and Recall in African American Children." *Journal of Black Psychology* 24 (4): 455–475.

Beneke, Margaret, and Gregory A. Cheatham. 2015. "Speaking up for African American English: Equity and Inclusion in Early Childhood Settings." *Early Childhood Education Journal* 43, no. 2 (March): 127–34.

Boutte, Gloria Swindler. 2016. *Educating African American Students: And How Are the Children?* New York: Routledge.

Breaux, Richard M. 2010. "After 75 Years of Magic: Disney Answers Its Critics, Rewrites African American History, and Cashes In on Its Racist Past." *Journal of African American Studies* 14 (4): 398–416.

Brittian, Aerika S., Adriana J. Umaña-Taylor, Richard M. Lee, Byron L. Zamboanga, Su Yeong Kim, Robert S. Weisskirch, Linda G. Castillo, Susan Krauss Whitbourne, Eric A. Hurley, Que-Lam Huynh, Elissa J. Brown, S. Jean Caraway. 2013.

"The Moderating Role of Centrality on Associations Between Ethnic Identity Affirmation and Ethnic Minority College Students' Mental Health." *Journal of American College Health* 61 (3): 133–40.

Byrd, Christy M. 2012. "The Measurement of Racial/Ethnic Identity in Children: A Critical Review." *Journal of Black Psychology* 38 (1): 3–31.

Clark, Kenneth B., and Mamie Clark. 1947. "Racial Identification and Preference in Negro Children." In *Readings in Social Psychology*, edited by T. M. Newcomb and E. L. Hartley, 169–78. New York: Holt.

Crenshaw, Kimberlé. 1989. "Demarginalizing the Intersection of Race and Sex: A Black Feminist Critique of Antidiscrimination Doctrine, Feminist Theory and Antiracist Politics." *University of Chicago Legal Forum* 1989 (1):139–67.

Crenshaw, Kimberlé. 1992. "Whose Story Is It Anyway? Feminist and Antiracist Appropriations of Anita Hill." In *Race-ing Justice, En-Gendering Power: Essays on Anita Hill, Clarence Thomas, and the Construction of Social Reality*, edited by Toni Morrison, 402–36. New York: Pantheon Books.

Davis, Judy Foster. 2018. "Selling Whiteness?—A Critical Review of the Literature on Marketing and Racism." *Journal of Marketing Management* 34 (1–2): 134–77. https://doi.org/10.1080/0267257X.2017.1395902.

Derman-Sparks, Louise, and Julie Olsen Edwards. 2010. *Anti-Bias Education for Young Children and Ourselves.* Washington, DC: National Association for the Education of Young Children.

Donohue, Chip, and Roberta Schomburg. 2017. "Technology and Interactive Media in Early Childhood Programs: What We've Learned from Five Years of Research, Policy, and Practice." *Young Children* 72, no. 4 (September): 72–78.

Dunbar, Angel D., Esther M. Leerkes, Stephanie I. Coard, Andrew J. Supple, and Susan Calkins. 2017. "An Integrative Conceptual Model of Parental Racial/Ethnic and Emotion Socialization and Links to Children's Social-Emotional Development among African American Families." *Child Development Perspectives* 11 (1): 16–22.

Dunham, Yarrow, Elena V. Stepanova, Ron Dotsch, and Alexander Todorov. 2015. "The Development of Race-Based Perceptual Categorization: Skin Color Dominates Early Category Judgments." *Developmental Science* 18 (3): 469–83. https://doi.org/10.1111/desc.12228.

Edwards, Jan R., and Peggy Rosin. 2016. "A Prekindergarten Curriculum Supplement for Enhancing Mainstream American English Knowledge in Nonmainstream American English Speakers." *Language, Speech, and Hearing Services in Schools* 47 (2): 113–122.

Escayg, Kerry-Ann, Rachel Berman, and Natalie Royer. 2017. "Canadian Children and Race: Toward an Anti-Racism Analysis." *Journal of Childhood Studies* 42 (2): 10–21.

Essien, Idara, and J. Luke Wood. 2021. "I Love My Hair: The Weaponizing of Black Girls Hair by Educators in Early Childhood Education." *Early Childhood Education Journal* 49, no. 3 (May): 401–12.

Halberstadt, Amy G., Alison N. Cooke, Pamela W. Garner, Sherick A. Hughes, Dejah Oertwig, and Shevaun D. Neupert. 2020. "Racialized Emotion Recognition Accuracy and Anger Bias of Children's Faces." *Emotion*: 1–15.

Hamlen, Karla R., and Krista J. Imbesi. 2020. "Role Models in the Media: A Content Analysis of Preschool Television Programs in the U.S." *Journal of Children and Media* 14 (3): 302–23. https://doi.org/10.1080/17482798.2019.1689369.

Hindley, Anna F., and Julie Olsen Edwards. 2017. "Early Childhood Racial Identity—The Potential Powerful Role for Museum Programing." *Journal of Museum Education* 42 (1): 13–21.

Howard, Tyrone C. 2018. "Capitalizing on Culture: Engaging Young Learners in Diverse Classrooms." *Young Children* 73, no. 2 (May): 24–33.

Kemple, Kristen M., Il Rang Lee, and Michelle Harris. 2016. "Young Children's Curiosity about Physical Differences Associated with Race: Shared Reading to Encourage Conversation." *Early Childhood Education Journal* 44 no. 2 (March): 97–105. https://doi.org/10.1007/s10643-014-0683-0.

King, Elizabeth K. 2021. "'You're Okay' May Not Be Okay." *Young Children* 76, no. 1 (March): 14–19.

Kohn, Shanna, Kim Foulds, Katie Maeve Murphy, and Charlotte F. Cole. 2020. "Creating a Sesame Street for the Syrian Response Region: How Media Can Help Address the Social and Emotional Needs of Children Affected by Conflict." *Young Children* 75, no. 1 (March): 32–41.

Kuh, Lisa, Debbie LeeKeenan, Heidi Given, and Margaret R. Beneke. 2016. "Moving Beyond Anti-Bias Activities: Supporting the Development of Anti-Bias Practices." *Young Children* 71, no. 1 (March): 58–65.

Lei, Ryan F., and Marjorie Rhodes. 2021. "Why Developmental Research on Social Categorization Needs Intersectionality." *Child Development Perspectives* 15 (3): 143–47.

Lemish, Dafna, and Colleen Russo Johnson. 2019. *The Landscape of Children's Television in the US & Canada*. New York: The Center for Scholars and Storytellers.

Love, Hailey R., and Margaret R. Beneke. 2021. "Pursuing Justice-Driven Inclusive Education Research: Disability Critical Race Theory (DisCrit) in Early Childhood." *Topics in Early Childhood Special Education* 41 (1): 31–44. https://doi.org/10.1177/0271121421990833.

MacNaughton, Glenda, Karina Davis, and Kylie Smith. 2010. "Working and Reworking Children's Performance of 'Whiteness' in Early Childhood Education." In *Imagining Children Otherwise: Theoretical and Critical Perspectives on Childhood Subjectivity*, edited by Michael O'Laughlin and Richard T. Johnson, 135–55. Vol. 46 of *Rethinking Childhood*, edited by Gaile Cannella. New York: Peter Lang, 1998– .

Masci, David, Besheer Mohamed, and Gregory A. Smith. 2018. "Black Americans Are More Likely than Overall Public to Be Christian, Protestant." Pew Research Center. April 23. www.pewresearch.org/fact-tank/2018/04/23/black-americans-are-more-likely-than-overall-public-to-be-christian-protestant.

Mbilishaka, Afiya M., and Danielle Apugo. 2020. "Brushed Aside: African American Women's Narratives of Hair Bias in School." *Race Ethnicity and Education* 23 (5): 634–53. https://doi.org/10.1080/13613324.2020.1718075.

Muhammad, Gholnecsar E., and Sherell A. McArthur. 2015. "'Styled by Their Perceptions': Black Adolescent Girls Interpret Representations of Black Females in Popular Culture." *Multicultural Perspectives* 17 (3): 133–40.

Park, Caryn C. 2011. "Young Children Making Sense of Racial and Ethnic Differences: A Sociocultural Approach." *American Educational Research Journal* 48 (2): 387–420. https://doi.org/10.3102/0002831210382889.

Perszyk, Danielle R., Ryan F. Lei, Galen V. Bodenhausen, Jennifer A. Richeson, and Sandra R. Waxman, 2019. "Bias at the Intersection of Race and Gender: Evidence from Preschool-Aged Children." *Developmental Science* 22 (3):e12788. https://doi.org/10.1111/desc.12788.

Price, Chris Lauren, and Elizabeth A. Steed. 2016. "Culturally Responsive Strategies to Support Young Children with Challenging Behavior." *Young Children* 71, no. 5 (November): 36–43.

Quinn, Paul C., Kang Lee, Olivier Pascalis, and James W. Tanaka. 2016. "Narrowing in Categorical Responding to Other-Race Face Classes by Infants." *Developmental Science* 19, no. 3 (May): 362–71. https://doi.org/10.1111/desc.12301.

Salinas-González, Irasema, María G. Arreguín-Anderson, and Iliana Alanís. 2018. "Supporting Language: Culturally Rich Dramatic Play." *Teaching Young Children* 11, no. 2 (December/January): 4–6.

Schmiesing, Ann. 2016. "Blackness in the Grimms' Fairy Tales." *Marvels & Tales* 30 (2): 210–233.

Souto-Manning, Mariana, and Ayesha Rabadi-Raol. 2018. "(Re)Centering Quality in Early Childhood Education: Toward Intersectional Justice for Minoritized Children." *Review of Research in Education* 42, no. 1 (March): 203–25. https://doi.org/10.3102/0091732X18759550.

Sturdivant, Toni Denese. 2021a. "Complying and Resisting: A Qualitative Metasynthesis of the Race and Gender Discourses Found in the Play of Young Children." *Journal of Educational Studies and Multidisciplinary Approaches* 1 (2): 84–104. https://doi.org/10.51383/jesma.2021.10.

Sturdivant, Toni Denese. 2021b. "Racial Awareness and the Politics in Play: Preschoolers and Racially Diverse Dolls in a US Classroom." *International Journal of Early Childhood* 53: 139–57. https://doi.org/10.1007/s13158-021-00289-5.

Sturdivant, Toni Denese, and Iliana Alanís. 2019. "Teaching through Culture: One Teacher's Use of Culturally Relevant Practices for African American Preschoolers." *Journal for Multicultural Education* 13 (3). https://doi.org/10.1108/jme-03-2019-0019.

Sturdivant, Toni Denese, and Iliana Alanís. 2021. "I'm Gonna Cook My Baby in a Pot": Young Black Girls' Racial Preferences and Play Behavior. *Early Childhood Education Journal* 49, no. 3 (May): 473–82. https://doi.org/10.1007/s10643-020-01095-9.

Sullivan, Patricia. 2020. "Discovering the Brilliance and Beauty in Black." *Voices of Practitioners* 15 (Fall): 54–61.

Tominey, Shauna L., Elisabeth C. O'Bryon, Susan E. Rivers, and Sharon Shapses. 2017. "Teaching Emotional Intelligence in Early Childhood." *Young Children* 72, no. 1 (March): 6–14.

Triska, Zoë. 2017. "The Real Stories Behind These Disney Movies Will Ruin Your Childhood." *Huffington Post*. December 6. www.huffingtonpost.com/2013/11/12/the-real-story-behind-eve_n_4239730.html.

Van Ausdale, Deborah, and Joe R. Feagin, 2001. *The First R: How Children Learn Race and Racism*. Lanham, MD: Rowman & Littlefield Publishers.

Wanless, Shannon B., and Patricia A. Crawford. 2016. "Reading Your Way to a Culturally Responsive Classroom." *Young Children* 71, no. 2 (May): 8–15.

Weldon, Tracey L. 2000. "Reflections on the Ebonics Controversy." *American Speech* 75 (3): 275–77.

White, Aisha, and Shannon B. Wanless. 2019. "P.R.I.D.E.: Positive Racial Identity Development in Early Education." *Journal of Curriculum, Teaching, Learning and Leadership in Education* 4 (2): 73–84.

Winkler, Erin N. 2009. "Children Are Not Colorblind: How Young Children Learn Race." *PACE: Practical Approaches for Continuing Education* 3 (3): 1–8.

Winkler, Erin N. 2012. *Learning Race, Learning Place—Shaping Racial Identities and Ideas in African American Childhoods*. New Brunswick, NJ: Rutgers University Press.

Wright, Brian L. 2019. "Black Boys Matter: Strategies for a Culturally Responsive Classroom." *Teaching Young Children* 12, no. 4 (April/May): 20–22.

Wynter-Hoyte, Kamania, and Mukkaramah Smith. 2020. "'Hey, Black Child. Do You Know Who You Are?' Using African Diaspora Literacy to Humanize Blackness in Early Childhood Education." *Journal of Literacy Research* 52 (4): 406–31. https://doi.org/10.1177/1086296X20967393.

Zirkel, Sabrina, and Tabora Johnson. 2016. "Mirror, Mirror on the Wall: A Critical Examination of the Conceptualization of the Study of Black Racial Identity in Education." *Educational Researcher* 45 (5): 301–11. https://doi.org/10.3102/0013189X16656938.

INDEX